The Juggling Book

The Juggling Book

by Carlo

Vintage Books
A Division of Random House
New York

Library of Congress Cataloging in Publication Data
Carlo.
The Juggling Book.
1. Jugglers and juggling.
I. Title.
GV1559.C37 793.8 73-11411
ISBN 0-394-71956-5
Manufactured in the United States of America

Vintage Books Edition
1974

Jacket and book design by Ira Teichberg.

Contents

Introduction

Juggling Background

Juggling first became a part of my life late one summer afternoon in a resort in the Pocono Mountains in Pennsylvania. I was about twelve, and a man came over to where my brother and I were playing, picked up three apples and began to juggle them. He remarked that W. C. Fields learned to juggle using apples, and then he walked away, leaving me absolutely flabbergasted. How could an ordinary man like that juggle? It was amazing. I had no idea how he did what he was doing, and I had no way of finding out. But I was stuck on juggling.

The next summer I spent with my parents, who were doing publicity for a summer theater on Long Island. I hung around backstage and watched rehearsals. There were many parties and picnics for the cast and crew, and I remember one where all the actors were in very high spirits, joking, storytelling, and reciting monologues from old plays they had done. Others were doing stunts, standing on their hands, tumbling, and juggling. This second exposure to juggling was enough to make me determined to learn it regardless of how long or how much effort it took.

I tried to juggle at every opportunity, even though I still didn't know how to do it. One day my brother and I stood facing each other, and using one hand only, we got three croquet balls going between us. Each of us was one hand of a juggler. This is when I discovered how the throws were supposed to go. All I had to do next was figure out how to get the whole thing into my own two hands. I worked at it for days at the beach. One day it happened. I was throwing beer cans, and all of a sudden I found myself *doing* it! The cans were going by themselves. Much later I found out that beer cans were about the most difficult things I could have chosen to juggle with. From then on, apples, oranges, potatoes, and balled-up socks were not safe when I was around.

Juggling became my obsession and one of my personal trademarks, and I began to teach anyone who would give it a try, including my perennial summer girl friend. At one time we were using croquet balls, and in two days she was far ahead of me. We were measuring skill by how many throws we could do before we dropped the balls. She could do about 120 throws; I could do 20 or 25. My style was really poor—my hands and arms were flying all over the place, and I ran all over the room after the balls, never stopping juggling until I had dropped all of them. But at least I could keep the balls going for a while, and that was the only thing that counted.

Much, much later—around twenty years or so—I came across a circus group in Central Park doing all sorts of tumbling, clowning, and juggling. They were dressed up in commedia dell'arte costumes and called their group the Circo dell'Arte, giving the feeling of medieval troubadours. After the performance I talked with their leader, Hovey Burgess, who told me he ran a circus school called the Circus Arts Institute. He had run away from home at seventeen to join the circus, and by the time I met him, he was a veteran juggler and trapeze artist with many years of experience with various circuses, including Ringling Brothers. I showed up at his school the next day for my first class. The school was in a storefront on the Bowery, and when I pushed the door open, there was Hovey, sitting in an old barber chair in the midst of a pile of props, costumes, and equipment. (After he decided to take me under his wing, he dubbed me Carlo Ludovico, which was my name in Italian. The name stuck, and I still sometimes perform under the name Carlo. I call the teaching method I use the Carlo Method.)

Every class began with about a half-hour of free-style juggling, with Hovey going around helping people individually. Then came a half-hour of warm-up exercises. It always ended with a period of special instruction in some circus art such as bongo-board (rolling cylinder), stilts, balancing, slack-wire, unicycle, handstands, tumbling, or trapeze—my favorite. As time went on, word of mouth brought more and more people to the classes. Professional jugglers came to the school to practice, keep in shape, learn new tricks, and even teach us what they knew. (Jugglers, unlike some other performers, are always ready

3

to share their skills openly.)

Hovey Burgess impressed me deeply. On the surface, he had a kind of childlike way with us, but underneath he showed himself to be a very serious and dedicated man of the circus, a true performer, and a true teacher. He knew more about our bodies than we did, and he could show us how to make ourselves do what we needed to do.

During the two years that I studied with Hovey Burgess, I experienced many changes in my awareness. In the beginning my juggling "ability" was more of a "liability." I had to unlearn everything I had taught myself and then relearn from scratch. For the first few weeks I was so afraid of the trapeze I wouldn't go near it. I didn't do tumbling because of a condition in my right leg. But as time went on, I was able to overcome all my fears. I learned to tuck in my bad leg when tumbling, got used to going on the trapeze, and learned ball, hoop, and club juggling so well that I was soon teaching newcomers in the class. After a few months of hard work I was throwing double and triple club turns and passing clubs with partners just like anyone else there did.

A rapport began to develop among some of us who had started with Hovey at about the same time. A group of us began to develop our own routines, which led to the formation of a performing group we called Circus Minimus. The name suggested a certain modesty —in our skills, our style, and our expectations. We wanted spontaneity; we wanted to be able to go to Central Park or out on the streets *with* the people, not separated from them by make-up, costumes, expensive equipment, or flashy skills. Our motto was: "Another disaster by Circus Minimus," and much too often that was the case.

We got the equipment we needed from laundromats and garbage cans—bleach bottles and broomsticks, which we made into good, cheap clubs for juggling. We also made our own stilts, walking around New York City on them. People almost never failed to respond to us; we were hard to ignore. Our troupe of eight or ten went to peace rallies, schools, fairs, block parties, rock concerts, and Easter, Earth Day, and Eclipse celebrations. We juggled in the rain, as well as in the sun, and we performed on buses, subways, and even in restaurants, sometimes for four or five hours straight.

Circus Minimus became increasingly "minimus," until finally I was the only remaining person. However, I continued to teach juggling in the churchyard of Trinity Church in New York twice a week during lunch hour. Anyone who came by to gawk was invited to take a lesson. Hundreds of people accepted my offer, and quite a few stayed with me for many months and became good jugglers. An accountant made a beautiful set of clubs and juggled them while doing a soft-shoe number in a little demonstration performance we arranged. Three young women from New Jersey practiced extra hours and came up with some surprisingly good and original ball-bouncing variations. One thing became certain: No one was ever quite the same after an encounter with juggling.

The sequence of activities that I call the "Juggling Experience" has many benefits for anyone willing to work conscientiously. Juggling tones and strengthens various parts of your body—your hands, wrists, and arms, your nervous system, and especially your eyes. Coordination, which is not an innate quality but just another skill to be learned, will be sharpened, bringing your whole body into a heightened state of awareness. Juggling will also help you to gain proper organization and control of your body energies. Even picking up the balls you drop can help you to take off some of that extra poundage around your midsection!

Working intensely on any new skill can have a healing effect on your psyche. There is satisfaction in working hard to achieve new skills and pleasure in exhibiting them to others. It can be a delightful experience to work through a spot on which you have been stuck and to reach a new level of ability. Then, of course, once you have attained a certain degree of skill, you will find that there is no better way to relax after a hard day's work than to spend a half-hour juggling. My experiences on Wall Street demonstrated the wonderful relaxing effects that juggling had on the office workers who joined my classes during their lunch hour. In fact, a "juggling break" can be just as relaxing, cheaper, and better for you than a "drug break" for coffee or tobacco.

Working with a partner is a great experience, especially if he or she is a friend or a member of your family. The adjustment of partners to one another's rhythm and style is good practice in learning cooperation and sensitivity to another person's needs. Three, four, or even more jugglers can learn to work together harmoniously in a single group formation. When you perform your hard-earned skills before others, you can experience the pleasure of giving them something from very deep within yourself. Teaching others and leading them through this learning and growing experience is not for everyone, but for those who feel the gift in themselves, it can be a real adventure for both teacher and student.

On a still higher level, juggling is a meeting ground for various arts and skills: theater, dance, mime, physical culture, and sport. Even sculpture and music can be related to juggling. Sculptors and other artists see in the juggler's body a beautiful synthesis of form and motion, economy of energy, minimum movement, solidity, calmness, balance, equilibrium, and the control and direction of body forces. Many actors, dancers, and even singers have studied with both Hovey Burgess and myself to develop these qualities, including rhythm and group tuning, and use them in their own work. Musicians have found juggling useful for strengthening their hands and warming up before practicing or performing.

Finally, the Juggling Experience, presented here through the Carlo Method, can teach you to remember yourself, observe what you do with your body, center yourself, calm your mind and thoughts, let your emotions subside, monitor your inner state, and generate physical energy and power. This level of awareness can bring you into contact with the "music of the spheres," or more accurately for juggling, the "rhythm of the spheres."

The history of juggling goes back to ancient Egypt and probably much earlier times. Carvings of jugglers have been found in the ruins of ancient civilizations, such as the pre-Columbian era in the New World. Alexander the Great was entertained by jugglers after his great victories. There are also the ritual acrobats and jugglers of Persia and the sudden reappearance of jugglers, mimes, and jesters during the rebirth of consciousness in Europe called the Renaissance. The court fool, usually a juggler, had the privilege of saying anything about the king in his presence and in front of everyone, since he was, after all, just a fool.

Right now, in this country, we are experiencing another rebirth of consciousness, which some people call the New Age. In addition, there has been a new flowering of interest in spontaneous street theater, mime, juggling, and other circus and performing arts.

We are seeing today more emphasis on the real and less on the artificial and plastic; more stress is given to private meditation and simple, open, direct relationships. With this has come an enthusiasm for spontaneous activities and entertainments and a strong emphasis on the development of genuine and personal skills. In my juggling work, I de-emphasize the old image of the wiseacre, bow-tie-wearing, silk-hatted juggler in tuxedo or tails equipped with gimmickry and frills such as lampshades, knives, bottles, torches, and cups and saucers in favor of the simplicity of basic skills involving pure shapes—balls, clubs, and hoops. I believe in relying on hard work and dedication to the art, rather than clever deception, and in creating an open relationship with my audience when I perform.

It is my intention here to demythologize juggling. I would like to see juggling go from the circus ring to the front yard, to become something to *do,* something to get involved in, rather than merely something to watch. Juggling could easily become a national craze: It is easy to learn (even young children can learn to juggle as soon as they can throw and catch a ball); it is adaptable for partners and groups; and it is competitive. Equipment is cheap, easy to make, and portable. There are great possibilities for creativity, with hundreds of original patterns and variations.

This book is a summary of the things I have been saying to my students. Some of you will use it to learn "how to juggle" and will let it go at that, which is fine. The book is directed to that end, with a wealth of detailed hints and instructions; the way is completely charted for you. Others might be interested in going further, into advanced and partner work, performing, and teaching. These areas are covered also. Still others will see and experience the changes in consciousness I spoke of earlier. These too are here, but they will be revealed only through dedicated inner work. Each of you will find the level at which you can work best. I only wish I could work with each of you personally, but this of course is not possible. All I can do is lead you through the Juggling Experience and hope that each of you finds what he or she wants there. I hope that you will enjoy yourselves, discover joy and satisfaction in this ancient form of amusement, body training, and conscious activity and that you will keep a glow in your heart whenever you juggle.

The Carlo Method

Juggling is not really as hard as most people seem to think it is. It is something that everyone can learn how to do—like running, whistling, or riding a bicycle. Once learned, the ability to juggle is never lost or forgotten, no matter how young or old you are when you learn or how many years intervene. In my teaching experience I have never found anyone unable to learn because of any so-called lack of coordination. This is a myth that conveniently covers up a real desire to learn, embarrassment, or some other kind of mental block. If you can throw and catch a ball, you can learn how to juggle.

Basis of the Method. The heart of the Carlo Method lies in working with the consciousness and inner awareness of the juggler. You facilitate this by doing your work in very small units or tasks. These are given one at a time and must be watched closely and done carefully. Each task should be performed "perfectly" a prescribed number of times before moving on to the next step. Each task is designed to prepare you for the next, which is just a little bit harder. Although it may not always be obvious, each task has a purpose, such as helping you to get rid of certain common habits that might interfere with your further progress. For this reason, nothing should be skipped.

How to Work. Juggling *appears* to be a very complex thing. It looks as if you are doing a lot of things at the same time. The Carlo Method is set up in small tasks so that each motion, each unit of energy, and each position of the body can be looked at clearly and experienced. This is somewhat like an "exploded" diagram of a machine in which the parts are drawn strung out in all directions. The Carlo Method presents in an "exploded" form the steps of learning how to juggle. Each task assigned is easy enough for you to see clearly just what you have to do and be able to do it. You really shouldn't get stuck anywhere. When you have only a small piece to work on at a time, you can catch errors and correct them very quickly.

If I said to you, "Climb a mountain," there would be many wrong ways you could go about doing it. But if I showed you how to walk, how to breathe, how to pace your energy, how to keep your footing, and all the other details of climbing, you could work on these things separately, put them all together, and then go climb the mountain. In the same way, if I told you, "Throw the balls," or even if I told you the paths that the balls should take, this would be too big a piece for you to work on. You might get started, but after a few throws you would probably have balls flying all over the room without knowing what to do about it. In the Carlo Method you begin by throwing just one ball. When you have mastered the eight or nine points at this level, you can then move on to the next level.

I can't check each of you personally as you do each task, but I do strongly advise you to work slowly, taking enough time to learn each step perfectly. In that way you will not reinforce or pick up bad habits that will later expand into major blocks, making it harder for you to learn juggling than when you began. Of course, it may be that you can do some of these steps perfectly the first time. Nevertheless, work on them awhile, making sure that you stop to experience and feel what you are doing with your body and also with your mind.

Let your whole being slow down so that you can see what is happening. Then move on to the next step.

Some people are "naturals" and learn simple three-ball juggling very quickly. However, this is of little further use if they have not gained control of their bodies and energies. Without this control, juggling will be as hard for them as if they knew nothing at all about it. Beware of becoming satisfied with a mere crumb when a whole loaf stands waiting for you.

Keep the work pure: Do not experiment with or invent other types of throws, catches, or sequences until you have been told you are ready to do so. You should never even play with the objects you juggle with or toss them around casually. They are the sacred objects of the discipline; they should not be subjected to thumb-twiddling or fidgeting. Such fooling around may create vibrations that are out of tune with the work you are doing, and you may destroy the fine, subtle tuning that is supposed to be taking place in your body and mind as you work.

Using This Book. Everything you need to know is in this book. Make sure that you read every word carefully as you work through each lesson. Do not let anything slip by that you do not understand or cannot do with sat-isfaction. You will find the instructions outlined in extremely fine detail, giving you enough information to help answer any question that might arise about some aspect of your work. Don't preread the book, for you will only confuse yourself. It is not a novel; it is a manual for *doing* something. Read and reread each lesson as you do the things described. Then you will be on your way to becoming a juggler. It might help if you had a friend read aloud to you from the book so that your hands could be free to practice the particular exercise. This is especially helpful in sections where much new material is covered. Your friend might want to learn juggling with you, and the two of you can work together as partners.

"Spectatorism." Many people come to me while I am teaching and want to watch. Others want to get into long, involved discussions about what juggling is and what it means. I tell these people politely that the experience of juggling is not in the mind, the imagination, or words, or even in the eyes. All the talking in the world, or even reading this book, will not alone make the balls do their cosmic dance. The experience of juggling is *in* the juggling; your hands must become involved. In order to know what juggling is all about, you have to *do* it, and you can only do it with your hands.

I.
Basic
Cascade
Ball
Juggling

Cascade Juggling

Juggling has traditionally been compared to the flow of water, and from that analogy some of the terms in juggling have been derived. One of these terms is "Cascade" juggling, which refers to the way that the three balls ascend in the center and come down on the outside, like water cascading in a fountain. Sometimes the word "fountain" is used.

Equipment. The very first step in learning to juggle is to get equipment. Since ball juggling is the first and easiest juggling to learn, I will consider it first. The balls should be solid but able to bounce well. Each ball should have enough weight so that when it hits your palm it forces your hand to close partway around it. For better visibility, it is best for the balls to be white, and they should be washable. The balls that best fit this description are lacrosse balls. They cost about one dollar each. If you are planning to take up juggling in a serious way, I recommend that you get six of these balls. In any case, get three. If you can't find lacrosse balls, the next best are dog balls, which bounce well and come in colors. These are available in most well-stocked pet shops.

If you get white balls, you should also get a few balls in other colors. Colored balls will be useful for certain exercises in this book where a marked ball will be called for. For simplicity, the marked ball will always be referred to as the "red" ball, even though the colored ball you use for this may not be red.

If you cannot get lacrosse or dog balls, some alternatives are: baseballs (a little too big; the weight is all right, but they do not bounce); sponge balls (the size is fine, but they are a little too light, and the bounce is weak); or tennis balls (these are fine for the first few lessons, but are too light for advanced work, and fly away too easily). Golf balls and handballs are too small.

If possible, get the best equipment that you can find, and save yourself some unnecessary work. But remember that it is possible—after you have become a skilled ball juggler—to use any objects for juggling. I learned with beer cans. You can start working with stones, fruit of various kinds (oranges are the best), knobs, eggs (boiled first, later raw), handkerchiefs, balled-up socks, cans, and so on. Later you can even try using a combination of objects of different size and weight. For example, you can try juggling with a regular lacrosse ball, a ping-pong ball, and a lead sinker. Right now though, and for some time to come, you should work with three lacrosse balls. You will need everything in your favor that you can get.

Lesson 1: Basic Position

At this point in the book, the various tasks that are a part of each lesson will be described, followed by a practice section summarizing the lesson and assigning the work. Before reading the next lesson you should do the exercises as they are given. In this way you will not become confused when I tell you to do something in Lesson 9 that is the exact opposite of what I told you to do in Lesson 1.

Body Orientation. First, before you start juggling, get yourself in tune with the place where you will be working. Pick a room in which there are not too many pieces of furniture. You don't want to be fishing balls out from under sofas and chairs. Remove any breakable items. Close windows if there is any possibility of a ball going outside and causing damage or getting lost. It is more difficult to work and to concentrate outdoors, but it is possible.

Choose a good flat wall, and stand facing it, about six or eight feet from it. Stand square with the room. Now look around and familiarize yourself with everything in the room so that you can concentrate on your juggling without being distracted by anything. Children or animals may be distracting and be a hazard to your work—or possibly, your work may be hazardous to them. Next, be sure that you are in your "spot." Be aware of the floor under your feet and the ceiling and walls around you, and try to relate your center to them. The floor, walls, and ceiling are reference points that help you to determine your position and balance.

Wall Plane. Now look at the wall in front of you, and imagine a series of planes parallel to that wall, like a series of screens set up in front of you. One of those imaginary planes passes about a foot in front of you, making you feel as if you were standing only a foot from the wall. That plane is called the "Wall Plane." It is an essential part of the Carlo Method, and I will be referring to it often in the course of these lessons.

Body Position. Stand erect, facing the wall, with your body, especially your shoulders, relaxed. Swing your arms a few times to relax them, and then let them dangle. Take several deep breaths slowly in and out. Close your eyes for a second, and clear your mind of distractions. Set your mind to think only about the work at hand. The only thing you should be conscious of is your juggling and how your body feels and responds to it. Free your whole body from tension, especially your head, neck and shoulders. Tension blocks the free flow of energy, which is vital to juggling. You will find, as you proceed, that one of the things the art of juggling depends on is good, clearly defined charges of energy being sent to your hands at the right time and in the right quantity. Tension will only hinder this flow. Once you have learned to juggle, you will discover that it can function as a barometer of your inner state. In my own experience I have learned that it is impossible for me to do certain complex variations when I am tense about something, not really "there," or not in an open, positive frame of mind.

Notice the way your arms hang from your shoulders. Then notice the position of your elbows at your sides. Now slowly raise your forearms, with your elbows remaining in the same place they were. Bring your forearms up to level and keep them parallel to each other, shoulder-distance apart. Turn your hands palms up, imagining that you are carrying a tray of dishes, which, of course, has to be carried level at all times. It cannot be allowed to tilt even for a split second, or the dishes will slide off the tray in whatever direction you tilt it. It is the same with juggling. If your forearms

The Wall Plane

Home Position

do not remain level and parallel at all times, the balls will be all over the floor surprisingly quickly. Like the dishes, the balls will go toward the direction you tilt your forearms. For lack of a better term, this level plane will be referred to throughout this book as the "Tray Plane."

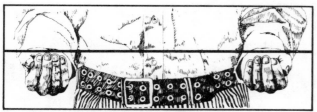

Tray Plane, showing position of arms

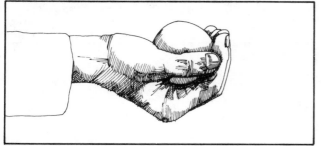

Cupped hand

Cup. While in this position, form a cup in each of your upturned hands. Imagine that you want to drink some water from a faucet but have no cup, and so you must make one with your hand. The sides of your cupped hand must be level so that the water won't spill out.

Home Position. When you have done all this, you are in "Home Position." If you are juggling properly, you should never have to depart from this position. Your upper arms should remain hanging straight, with your elbows at your sides. Neither your upper arms nor your elbows should move during normal juggling. Your lower arms and cupped hands should remain level. They will make some slight movements but must always return to Home Position. Your lower arms must remain parallel, and they should never enter the area directly in front of your stomach. Any closing-up gesture suggests weakness and receptivity; opening-up gestures—for example, your arms up and wide apart—suggest strength and assertion. Avoid weak gestures such as closing your hands or arms in front of your body or keeping your hands or feet too close together. A position too wide open also makes it extremely difficult to catch. Through experience I have found that the arms-parallel position is the ideal one for beginning juggling.

Home-Position Practice. Stand in Home Position, as described. Feel this pose awhile and become accustomed to it, so that you can tell automatically when you are in it and when you are not in it. Your body should be relaxed. Do not hold this position stiffly; use only the minimum energy to stay in it. Breathe naturally; don't hold your breath. Now swing your arms and your upper body around in various directions. After each swing return to Home Position without looking down at your arms to see where they are. At this stage, don't try to move your hands as if you were juggling, this will only create bad habits and take your attention from the work at hand.

Throughout your juggling you should always be in Home Position at the beginning of each volley. (A volley is a series of throws in a unit with a beginning and an end.) The goal is to be able to *stay* in Home Position throughout the entire volley. In the beginning you may be shifting out of Home Position, but as time goes on, you will learn to keep your lower body, starting with your feet, from moving. Later, your upper body, chest and shoulders, will remain still during the volley. Later still, your elbows will remain almost motionless. One goal of good juggling is to have your entire body remain perfectly still, so the balls do *all* the moving. This, of course, is actually impossible, but you should try to achieve this perfect stillness as much as you can. Your hands will be moving slightly, but the rest of your body will be relaxed and at rest, conserving its energy. Motion attracts attention, therefore you want the attention of those watching to go to the balls rather than to the juggler.

I will be referring to Home Position throughout these lessons. Your body too, without your conscious knowledge, will be continually referring itself to this basic centered position, once you have practiced it enough and it has become established in you as the normal stance for juggling.

Lesson 2: Basic Work & Self-Checking

Basic Throw. In this lesson and the few that follow, you will be working on the fundamental juggling pattern, which is called the "Regular Cascade." To make things as easy as possible for you, you will be working with only one ball during this entire lesson.

Take a ball and place it in your right hand. Don't grab or clutch it; just let it rest there, cradled by your hand. Your hand should form the Cup, as described in the previous lesson. This Cup should be loose so that the ball is very close to your fingers but doesn't actually touch them. Feel its weight. Become aware of its shape. During this work you should strive to experience each thing you do, not just with your mind but also with your body and all your senses.

The object of this lesson is to learn the proper way to throw a ball for juggling purposes. You may already be expert at throwing a ball for various games and sports. That is fine. Now I am asking you to forget temporarily *everything* you know about throwing and catching. Be in a state of mind where you are totally incapable of throwing a ball but are willing to learn. Then you will make rapid progress in juggling.

Popping. When you learned to throw a ball as a child, you allowed your wrist to break so that the ball rolled off your fingers. In the juggling throw, your wrist does not break. Instead the center of your hand pops up for a second so that the Cup that was there disappears for an instant and your hand becomes flat. As your hand flattens, your fingers should spread out, with your thumb and little finger as far apart as possible. The center of your hand drives the ball straight up. To aid in throwing the ball you can also use your wrist a little. The wrist makes a quick snap upward as you open your hand. Your forearm can also make a quick little motion upward. Both of these movements should cover only very short distances. The juggling term for this basic throw is "Popping."

Wind-Up and Follow-Through. Popping is quick, sudden, and short. There is no Wind-up (movement anticipating the throw) and there is no Follow-through (movement following the throw). Everything happens in an instant of time. The ball goes, but the hand hardly moves. The reason for this quick Popping is that in later work, where you are dealing with three or more balls at a quicker pace, there

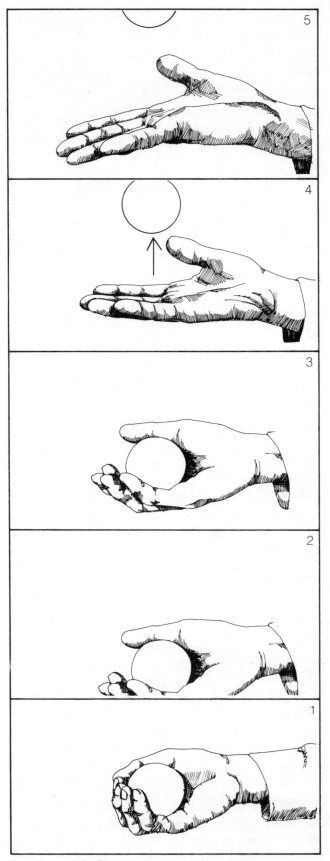

Popping the ball

will be no time for such extravagant movements as Wind-up and Follow-through. It is better to learn to do without these movements now.

Energy. In Popping, a charge of energy originates in your Energy Center, comes down your arm and out of your hand. Very little energy is used by your elbow and wrist. There should be no energy exerted in any other part of the body. (So-called body English is of no value in juggling—it wastes energy and makes you look ungraceful.) When Popping, be careful that the hand you are not using does not involuntarily jerk up and down while you are throwing with the other hand.

The instant of time in which the throw takes place is as long as it takes to snap your fingers. Before—nothing. After—nothing. It all happens in the moment of the throw. Don't anticipate. It's like the frog. He sits on the bank of a pond. Everything is still and quiet. Then suddenly—plop!—and he's gone. Everything is still and quiet again.

Sharpness and Mushiness. In the early work of juggling, your movements must be sharp and definite. Musicians would call it *marcato,* or marked rhythm. If you should see accomplished jugglers using a smoother rhythm, it is because, at a later time, the movements must be smoothed out. This will happen when you have learned each of the movements well, and when they have become so well defined and integrated that you can do them entirely without conscious attention. For the moment the task at hand is to keep out any overlapping flowing motion, or what I call mushiness. Later, at the proper point, you will be instructed how to add a flowing quality to your juggling. Earlier this flowing quality only serves to mask your errors and keeps you from seeing and correcting them.

The practice session for this lesson follows the section entitled "Self-Checking Methods." Please read that section first before starting on your practice.

SELF-CHECKING METHODS

In order to enable you to become your own teacher as soon as possible, without the need of another person to watch and comment on your work, the Carlo Method includes a number of Self-Checking techniques. Self-observation of Spin, Height, and the Wall and Tray Planes, and most important, the use of various Freeze techniques are included in these prescribed methods for Self-Checking.

Watching the Spin. This first method of Self-Checking will help show you how to throw properly. Most of the problems beginning jugglers have with incorrect throwing comes from breaking the wrist, which causes your fingers to trail along and "wipe" the ball as it leaves your hand. In this way of throwing, contact between your fingers and the ball lasts a long time. The direction in which the ball goes as it rolls off your hand is related to just how long this contact lasts and how much pressure is applied by your fingers. This way of throwing makes it very difficult to send a ball in exactly the same direction each time. When you are juggling with three or more balls, you have neither the time nor the attention available to watch and control where each ball goes. Also, putting a spin on the ball by rolling it in this fashion affects its flight as well as the way in which it is caught.

Watching the Spin is important because it directly indicates whether you are wiping the ball or correctly Popping it. Watch the ball as it reaches the top of its flight. It should not be turning over, but hanging motionless in the air. If it is rolling forward, you are probably pulling your elbow back as you throw and breaking the wrist, causing the ball to trail along the fingers. This Self-Checking method may also indicate that you are throwing the ball, not from the Cup you are supposed to use, but from the middle of your fingers. If should you see the ball rolling inward toward the center, it means that as you Pop it you are sliding your hand out from under the ball toward the outside. This is less common, but some people have a tendency to pour the ball out of their hand.

To help you detect this spinning, the balls you work with should have some distinct design on them. You can buy rubber balls with little designs painted on them in any toy store. If you are working with lacrosse balls, you can put thin strips of colored tape around them in various directions, which will enable you to see just when and how fast they are spinning.

If the ball is correctly popped out of your hand, it will not spin. This means that the push is being given at only one point, the point directly beneath the ball. The impetus or force should be straight up, just like the push given by the plunger of a pinball machine. The part of your hand that should be under the ball is the fleshy area running along the base of your fingers. No other part of your hand should be touching the ball. Do not rest the ball on your fingers themselves.

Try it and see. You will be able to feel the difference between rolling and popping. If you are holding your forearms level, in the Tray Plane, the popped ball can only go straight up. This is because a popped ball can only go at right angles to your forearm. If you hook the ball by hanging on to it too long, it will come toward your face and may go over your shoulder. If you let your hand go slack, the ball will go the other way, away from you. Work on this until you get the popping action to become natural, with no spin at all on the ball. Later you will have a lot of other things to think about, and the popping must go by itself.

Height. The next Self-Checking method is to consider the height you throw the balls. It stands to reason that if you want more time to think about what to do next, you can get it by throwing the balls higher. However, if you throw the balls too high, you will have to look up to see where they are, and you will forget where your hands are. Another problem that comes from throwing the balls too high is that the higher they are thrown, the further from you they are likely to come down. A good compromise is to keep the balls high enough to give you time to work, but low enough so that you can see everything that's going on. Imagine that there is a picture frame in front of you in which the juggling is going on. You must make sure that this picture frame is entirely within your area of vision.

A law of physics states that if you throw an object twice as high as another object, it takes *four* times as long to come down. To say this another way: If you were to throw a

Everything happens within the picture frame.

ball only half as high as you should, you would be robbed of three-quarters of the time that you need. Therefore height is an important factor in juggling.

To find the proper height at which to throw the balls, try this experiment. Wiggle your fingers around in various parts of your field of vision while looking straight ahead. You will notice that your vision cuts off sharply just above the top of your hairline. A good rule is: Throw the ball as high as the level between your eyes and the top of your head. Remember: You are not nine feet tall!

Tray Plane. You should avoid having your hands fly up to catch the balls. The balls will come down, which I can guarantee from long experience. Wait for them. Make your hands stay within the Tray Plane, and catch the balls only as they reach there. Letting your hands fly up above the level of the Tray Plane has the effect of cutting off the bottom of your picture frame or juggling pattern and robbing you of valuable time.

Wall Plane. There is another important plane —the Wall Plane, which I talked about earlier. Recall the feeling of the wall about one foot in front of you. As I explained, this plane is not the wall itself but the imaginary plane close to you. Making sure that the throwing of the balls takes place in this Wall Plane is an important Self-Checking technique.

The ball in the Cup of your right hand is in the Wall Plane. The rule here is: All balls in juggling stay in the Wall Plane. The balls never pass in front or in back of one another. They always move next to, above, or below one another, staying in the Wall Plane. It's as if you were washing a window with a rag in each hand. It wouldn't do any good to lift the rag off the window, and it would be even worse to push your hand through the pane of glass. Also, it wouldn't help if you started to wipe the back of one hand with the rag in the other hand. Up to this time, you have been conditioned to throw a ball to someone else. In juggling, of course, you are throwing the ball from your one hand to your other hand. All throwing takes place in this Wall Plane.

The Freeze. The most important Self-Checking technique, and perhaps the most unique and distinguishing part of the Carlo Method, is the "Freeze." There are actually a number of related Freeze techniques that you will be learning. These are similar to a certain "stop" exercise, to stop-motion photography, and to a children's game, which all of us would do well to play once in a while, known as either "Freeze" or "Red Light." In this game the leader calls "Green light!" and everyone goes about his business. When he calls "Red light!" everyone has to hold his position exactly as he was at that moment. If anyone moves after that, even the slightest, he did it wrong. Most of the time we are machines, and everything we do, especially physically, we do automatically. The only way that we can see this automatic behavior is to stop what we are doing and take a look. The Freeze technique helps to break up the work into small units and also stops the accumulating build-up of momentum in the energies of the body. The Freeze technique, almost single-handedly, has enabled me to teach people how to juggle in a few days, rather than in a number of weeks.

Freeze-on-Catching. This is the main Freeze technique. It is not easy. As you catch each ball, imagine that someone just called "Freeze!"

(1) When you hear this: Stop everything at the moment that the ball first makes contact with your hand. At that moment it's all over. Remain absolutely motionless, not only with your hands and arms perfectly still, but also every part of your body.

(2) Wait. No matter how ungraceful you are at the moment of Freeze, you must stay there. Wait three or four seconds at least, which should be long enough to let your mind catch up with your body. Work on not moving any part of your body after that instant of Freeze.

(3) Relax. Don't tense up in that position. Just lightly stop whatever you are doing at the moment of Freeze and hold it. Tensing up will only interfere with what you are trying to see and will get in the way of knowing what was really happening at that moment. Tensing up can be defined as using more energy to hold a position than you actually need. What you want is to use exactly the needed amount of energy and no more.

(4) Look. This three- or four-second waiting period will give you time for your mind to catch up with what your body was doing, and you will be able to examine the exact position of your body at the moment of Freeze and make the necessary corrections. Sometimes you will see something you can consciously correct. Sometimes it is better just to take a calm, unthinking look, letting your body make its own corrections. This is similar to what happens when you learn to ride a bicycle or drive a car. In the beginning, you have to think a lot. But soon, *you* do very little. By letting your body act alone, it will do most of what is necessary by itself.

The totality of juggling is so complex that you have to be able to take microscopic looks at what you are doing at each step along the way. The Freeze technique enables you to take an instant photograph of yourself at any moment, without even waiting ten seconds for the film to develop. If instead of the Freeze you go on moving after the critical moment, you will completely lose any notion of what you were actually doing at that moment. If you instantly pull the ball back to Home Position, without waiting to take a look at it, you will forget what you did that resulted in the bad throw, and the data will not be available for you to improve your work. So wait, and take a look.

(5)Return. After this waiting period, slowly return to Home Position. This motion will show you how much you departed from the Home Position. Remember that any departure from Home Position is an error; the greater the departure, the worse the error. You should always be careful to come back exactly to the same (Home) position each time. If you throw from a different position each time, you will be forever readjusting everything, and you will never be accumulating and building on a solid foundation of previous experience.

Horizontal Error. Let's analyze a typical throw: Suppose you froze with your left hand about a foot out to the left of its normal spot in Home Position. This means that you threw the ball to that location. Since this throw was with your *right* hand, the indication is that your right hand threw the ball too wide. The *throwing* hand is the guilty party in terms of errors within the Tray Plane, that is, Horizontal Errors.

Vertical Error. To take another example: If your left hand froze six inches *above* its normal spot in Home Position, it would mean that you brought your left hand up to meet the ball, instead of waiting for the ball to come down into your hand. In this case, the Freeze diagnoses vertical errors in the *catching* hand. If you Freeze with your hand very high, say near your shoulder, you should first move slowly in the direction the ball was going in order to see where it would have landed if you had waited for it to come down. Then return to Home Position. In this way, you can diagnose both Horizontal and Vertical Errors at the same time.

Body Freeze. Don't neglect the rest of your body in the Freeze. Check to see if your back is being twisted to one side or the other as you move around to catch a wide throw. If your back or knees are bent, it indicates that you waited too long to catch the ball and therefore you are catching it too low. If you Freeze having taken a step in some direction, you need to

work on bringing your throws in closer. It is especially important to correct movements in the lower body; the lower in the body a movement takes place, the more important it is to correct. In the beginning the Freeze will reflect a combination of many different errors, and soon you will be able to identify each of them separately and correct each one properly. The whole Freeze process, which I have just described, can be summarized as a repeated cycle: juggle; freeze (relax); wait; look; return; and juggle again. This basic Freeze-on-Catching technique will be called simply "Freezing" and will be referred to repeatedly throughout this book.

Freeze-on-Dropping. Another closely related technique is Freezing at the moment you drop a ball. This can be very useful in seeing exactly what you are doing at the moment of an error. When you drop a ball the important thing is to let it go and forget about it. The instant you know you have missed a ball, immediately stop and bring your attention back to *you*. At this point you should Freeze, using the above procedure for looking at yourself. Resist the temptation to go after the dropped ball. If you do, you will lose all the data about what *you* were doing at that moment.

Mid-air Freeze. This is a technique for later use that is very closely related to the other Freezes. Have a friend call out "Freeze" while you are juggling. Stop immediately. Let any balls not in your hands just *go*. Don't move a fraction of an inch anywhere. This is harder than it might seem at first—you will find you have a strong desire to grab the next ball. There is a powerful momentum in you that causes you to repeat an action, wrong or right, over and over again. This Freezing breaks that momentum and helps you to see what is happening.

Eyeball Freeze. This Freezing technique can only be used when watching another juggler. After he or she has begun to juggle, close your eyes for a few seconds. Open them suddenly, and then immediately close them again. You now have a photograph on your retina of what was happening, and you have about five or ten seconds to look at it. Do this in bright light, outdoors if possible. This technique will show you exactly where each ball was at the instant you focused on it. This is useful, like high-speed photography, for analyzing any complicated series of events. In juggling, Exchanges (to be explained later), Passing, and club juggling can all be seen better and analyzed by using the eyeball Freeze.

Basic Practice. This has been a long lesson. Many Self-Checking techniques have been introduced. Now you should try to integrate them into the work you were doing with one ball at the beginning of the lesson.

Place yourself in Home Position. Put a ball in your right hand, and form a Cup in each hand. Pop the ball back and forth between your two hands. Never hand or pass the ball across; always throw it upward, snapping your wrist. Throw the ball as high as your eyes or the top of your head. Keep your throws in the Wall Plane, and don't be afraid to throw near your face. Make the throws from your right and left hands equally high. Check the ball each time for Spin. Then

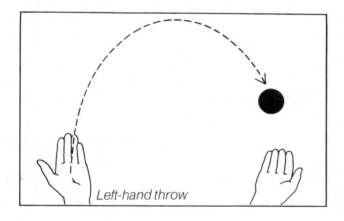
Left-hand throw

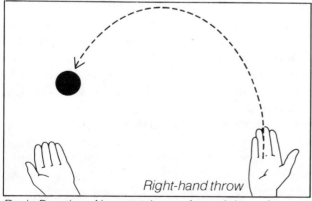
Right-hand throw

Basic Practice. Alternate throws from right and left hands

Freeze the instant you catch the ball and relax. Hold the Freeze three or four seconds as you observe and feel what happened. Slowly return your hands to Home Position, noting how far off you were. From Home Position throw the ball back the other way. Then repeat the procedure.

Always remember to keep your hands out of the central area in front of your stomach. Work toward staying in Home Position at all times. If the distance you cover with your hands in order to return to Home Position is *zero,* it indicates that you never left Home Position during the throw. This is what you are looking for. When you can do ten such perfect throws in a row, always staying in Home Position, and you have the feeling that you could continue to do this indefinitely, then you are ready to go on to the next lesson.

After you have mastered the Basic Practice, you can try juggling while sitting down with your elbows firmly touching your knees or legs. Also, you can strengthen your wrists by letting your opposite forearm rest on the wrist of the hand that is throwing the ball, thus preventing this wrist from flying upward.

If there is anything that you did not understand in the Basic Practice lesson, go back and read it again. Then do the exercises again. Do not short-change this lesson, for it contains probably 75 percent of all that you will need to know in order to learn to juggle. Perfect performance of the Basic Practice will put you well on the road to becoming a good juggler.

Lesson 3: One Throw

You might expect now to be given some exercises using two balls, but I have found it better most of the time to go right on to three. Two-ball exercises will be covered toward the end of the book, in the lessons on Two-Ball and Two-and-One juggling. Sometimes corrective exercises using two balls are given at this point.

Going right on to three balls will make you feel like a juggler. But right now you are not quite ready to throw all three of them; you will start by throwing just one ball of the three.

This lesson is designed to teach you how to begin and end a juggling volley. As soon as you pick up three balls with two hands, you will find that you have two balls in one hand and one in the other. The important thing to know is how to deal with two balls in one hand, both throwing (the beginning of a volley) and catching (the end of a volley).

Basket. You can no longer use the Cup, which you learned earlier, to hold two balls properly in one hand. Now you need a "Basket." First, make a Cup in your right hand and put a ball in it. While holding on to that ball, place a second one in the same hand. You will notice that you have to open your thumb, index finger, and middle finger in order to grasp the second ball. These three fingers form an open kind of basket around the second ball. One ball is in the center of your hand, and the second ball is out on your fingers. Do not slide the first ball toward your wrist unless it is absolutely impossible to hold the ball where it is. If you have small hands you should get smaller balls. There should be plenty of room for one ball in the center of your hand.

In this exercise, you will throw the fingertip ball in the Basket from one hand to the other. To do this you should form a Basket in each hand. The other two balls (one in the center of each hand) never move; they are just going along for the ride and are called "Riders." Except for the presence of these two Riders, everything here will be the same as in the Basic Practice. The Wall Plane passes through

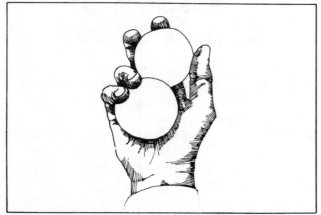

Holding two balls in a Basket

the fingers of each hand now, or more exactly, through the part of the Basket in which the thrown ball sits.

Basket Throw. This throw is still Popping. But since there is another ball in that hand, you will need more wrist-snap and elbow-snap to provide the energy for the throw. Remember to keep this snap fast, and make sure that your hand covers as little distance as possible. It will be of no use to lift your hand up and pour the ball out of it, as you would with sand. One approach to learning this throw is to do the Basic Practice, get the feeling of it, and then return to this One-Throw exercise, trying to duplicate the exact same feeling.

Basket Catch. The catch is a little tricky. The Basket is formed by four points of contact—your three fingers and the other ball. If the incoming ball hits the other ball before it hits your fingers, it will almost always bounce out. However, if the incoming ball touches your fingers first, there will be some "give" to cushion the impact. Then it can contact the other ball because your fingers are there to keep it from bouncing out. Never, never, let the Rider slide into your fingers. You should always catch and throw using the fingertips of your hand, and the Rider should always stay in your palm.

One-Throw Practice. Stand in Home Position. Relax. Put a ball in each hand. Put the third ball in your right hand on your fingertips, forming a Basket there. Make a Basket in your left hand also. Pop the ball back and forth from hand to hand. Keep it in the Wall Plane at all times. Throw to the same height in each direction, making the ball go up to eye level each time. Check the ball for Spin. Freeze on each catch: wait; look; return; and repeat. If you have problems, alternate this exercise with the Basic Practice. When this exercise looks and feels as good as the Basic Practice did, and you can do ten perfect throws in a row, go on to the next lesson.

In this lesson you have learned a new type of throwing and catching, how to use the Basket instead of the Cup, and how to handle the Riders.

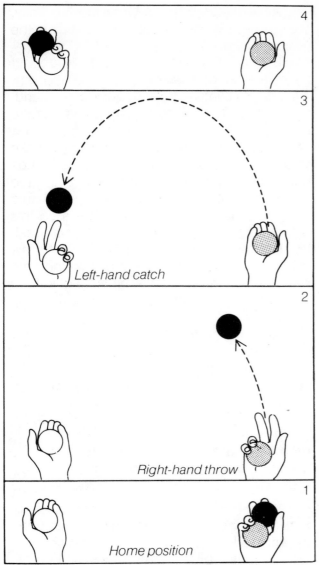

Left-hand catch

Right-hand throw

Home position

One-Throw Practice. Throwing one of three balls

Lesson 4: Two Throws

In this lesson you will be doing a volley of two throws, one from your right hand and one from your left. Although eventually you should be doing with your left hand everything that you do with your right, I am going to ask you always to begin with two balls in your right hand. This means that the first throw will always come from your right hand. Much later on, when you are an accomplished juggler, you can go back and start with two balls in your left hand. You will find that there will be almost nothing to learn by then, since your body has a way of automatically transferring most of what you have learned on one side to the other.

Since you are going to be doing two throws, you will end the volley with two balls in your right hand, just as you started it. You can form a Cup with your left hand because there will never be more than one ball in that hand at any time. With the two balls starting and ending in your right hand, you will have to keep a Basket there at all times.

To do Two Throws, proceed as follows: Throw a ball from your right hand as described in the last lesson. It goes up in the air, passes across your eyes, and falls toward your left hand. As the ball falls, but before it lands, your left hand pops its ball up under the incoming ball (an "Underthrow") and catches that first ball immediately. This second ball goes up across your eyes and down to your right hand. This is all there is to it. However, since this lesson is a crucial step on the path to juggling, I will analyze the various points in some detail.

Exchange. What happens over your left hand as you do this exercise is called an "Exchange." The first ball is coming into your left hand, but before it arrives you make room for it by emptying your left hand of its ball, which is thrown back the other way, under the incoming ball. One ball replaces the other, making an Exchange of balls.

Keep your juggling pattern really clean looking, and do not move all over the place to throw and catch the balls. The Exchange should be done in fairly close quarters.

Collisions. Most beginning jugglers have trouble with collisions. There is a simple way to avoid them. Throw the first ball so that it comes down *wide* of your left hand (toward the outside of your body). Throw the second ball from a point slightly inside, or to the right of your normal left-hand position, near the centerline of your body. After throwing, your left hand will move toward the outside to catch the incoming ball. (I rarely talk about catching, for it is instinctive to most people.) In brief: Throw *to* a point wide of your left hand, and throw *from* a point narrow of your left hand. A good guideline is that the ball should come

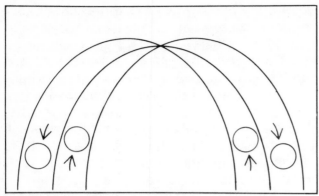

Traffic patterns in the air over the juggler's hands

down over your left thumb.

The two balls actually pass each other about four to eight inches above your left hand. The length of the Exchange is the total distance that the two balls are both in the air as they pass by each other. It can range from eight to fifteen inches, which means that when the incoming (first) ball is about eight inches above your left hand, the second ball starts to rise. A short Exchange means that the second ball is thrown late; a long Exchange means that the second ball is thrown early.

Traffic Problems. Visualize a highway coming down to your left hand. You will see the thrown ball going upward along the right side of the road and the incoming ball, like a car, will be coming at you in the other lane. If you throw the ball in the wrong direction, it will collide with the incoming ball. Also, the incoming ball will collide with you if it crosses the center-line of the highway.

The incoming ball will be on the wrong side of the road if you don't throw it wide enough from the right hand. This means that the incoming ball will be coming down directly on top of the ball in your left hand. At this point you have a number of choices, none of which will help you at all. They are as follows:

(1) You can just throw this second ball up toward the incoming ball, watch them collide, and then chase after both of them at the same time.

(2) You can get the second ball out of the way by rolling it forward off your fingers and letting the incoming ball fall into the back of your hand. This would violate all the principles of the Basic Practice. You would lose the pop-

ping action entirely, put a fantastic spin on the ball, and throw the ball straight ahead of you across the room.

(3) Another way to avoid a collision is to throw the second ball low, under the incoming ball, making it go straight across to the right hand. This is equivalent to veering off the highway into a ditch in order to avoid an oncoming car. Because of the energy relationships of such a low throw, the ball, like a bullet, will fly past your right hand, and probably into a closet full of dishes.

(4) Still another way of avoiding a collision is to swing your left hand, with its ball about to be thrown, down in a big arc in front of your stomach, to get clear of the incoming ball. This is contrary to the principle of keeping open the stomach area and the principle of minimum movement.

You can see from all these wrong alternatives that there is *nothing* you can do if you don't throw the first ball wide enough to the left hand. There will be no problem if you throw the first ball *wide,* so wide that if you didn't catch it with your left hand, it would drop on the floor, missing your hand entirely. Remember that there will be plenty of open air above your left hand for you to throw the second ball right up there where you've always thrown it.

Half Egg-Beater. Think again for a moment about the Exchange over the left hand. You will see that your left hand throws when it is at a point about an inch or so nearer the center-line of your body. That hand catches a moment later, as it moves to the outside of your body. Four things are happening: the throw; the move to the outside; the catch; and the move to the inside. Then the throw begins again, and so on. Since throwing is an upward action and catching is a downward action, this cycle produces a circular motion, which is similar to that of half an egg-beater. Do not exaggerate the circle. The motion is very small, not much larger than the diameter of the ball itself. It is more like a feeling than an actual motion.

Timing. One of the trickiest things about Two Throws is the timing. There are two separate throws and two separate catches.

Each of these four things happens at a different time. It isn't actually as complicated as that, since all catches are automatically taken care of (provided that you don't go up after the balls). You *must* catch a ball where it is; you have no choice. Just remember that each throw is a separate beat, a separate burst of energy. The rhythm is THROW . . . . wait . . . . THROW. The second throw comes at almost the very last possible moment before you catch the incoming ball. The second ball pops out of your left hand just before the first ball arrives from your right hand.

Don't throw the second ball too soon. If you throw it so soon that both balls are thrown at the same time, you will have to catch them at the same time, and it won't look very much like juggling. If you find yourself catching the two balls at the same time even though you threw them at different times, you are throwing the balls to different heights. Your right hand will be throwing the ball up to your head, and your left hand will be throwing only chest-high. The different times involved result in your catching both balls at the same time. This is not a coincidence. Your body finds it easier to catch both balls at the same time, and so it contrives to throw them in such a way that they come down together. The answer is to throw both balls to exactly the same height. Remember that if you let your hands go up after the balls, your timing will be seriously thrown off.

You should be aware of the rhythm, which consists of three exactly even-spaced beats: THROW • THROWCATCH • CATCH. The first catch is almost simultaneous with the second throw and is included in the same beat. The two constitute an Exchange, so the rhythm is really: THROW • EXCHANGE • CATCH. Examine your rhythm as you do this exercise. If you hear the rhythm: THROW • EXCHANGE . . . . CATCH, you can see that the second ball is being thrown too soon. You must simply wait longer before throwing it.

Don't throw too *late,* either. If you throw too late, the Exchange will be cut down to a few inches, and you will have hardly enough space to get the ball-to-be-thrown out from under the incoming ball. Also, you will be pressed for time. A telltale sign of this condi-

tion is if the left hand has to dip below the Tray Plane to catch the incoming ball. The only way you can get the necessary room for the Exchange is to borrow it from the space below the Tray Plane. The rhythm will also tell you: THROW . . . . THROW • CATCH. Experiment with throwing too soon and too late, just so you will be able to handle the situations and remedy them when they occur.

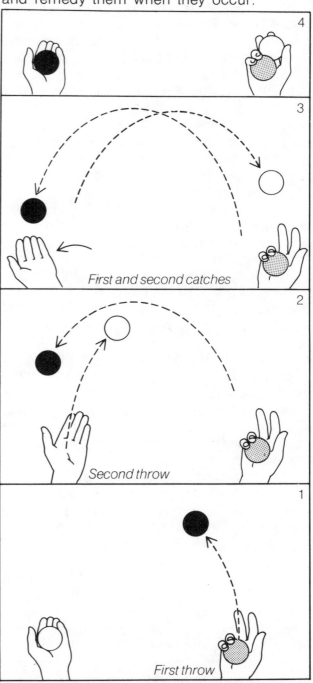

4

3

First and second catches

2

Second throw

1

First throw

Two-Throw Practice. Throw from right hand followed by throw from left

Two-Throws Freeze. In the more advanced lessons, the use of the Freeze becomes almost indispensable. When you have two balls to catch, you should freeze each hand separately as it catches its own ball. Freeze your left hand as it touches the first ball, and freeze your right as it touches the second. The position of each hand tells you how the other hand threw.

Two-Throws Practice. Stand in Home Position. Put two balls in your right hand, and one in your left. The ball in the Basket of your right hand and the ball in the Cup of your left are in the Wall Plane. Throw the first ball from your right hand; be sure to throw it wide, so that it lands to the left of your left hand. When this ball is about a foot above your left hand, pop the ball from your left hand *up under* the incoming ball. Throw it up to the same height and across to your right hand.

Always keep the balls in the Wall Plane. Do not let the two balls cross in front or in back of each other. Review the section on Traffic Problems to see if you are doing any of the wrong things listed there. Catch the first ball and freeze your left hand. Catch the second ball and freeze your right hand. Relax when you freeze, never tense up. Stop. Wait. Take a good look. Don't spend a lot of energy trying to figure out where you are at. Just take a look, and your body will make the corrections by itself. Return to Home Position, and repeat the procedure. If you have trouble catching both balls, make sure that you catch the first one and let the second one go — first things first.

Be careful that you don't get "mushy" when you are repeating the same action over and over. Avoid getting into a flow, expressive like modern dance. Make a definite break each time you return to Home Position, even if this means that your rhythm will look choppy. There will be time enough later to smooth it out. You are not doing muscle building, therefore the number of repetitions is not in itself very important. What is important is that you take a look at what you are doing each time. Doing the Freeze each time helps you break the accumulated momentum in your body. This momentum causes you to repeat whatever you are doing over and over again

in the same exact way. This can be a real hindrance. I call it the "Chewing-Gum Syndrome": Around and around and around, and it never goes anywhere. Make a definite break and begin fresh each time. Then any errors you make will be random rather than the same ones repeated again and again. If you let yourself repeat the same errors continually, you will be strengthening some very bad habits. Be very cautious about this. Always remember to look at yourself carefully at all times and catch your mistakes whenever you can.

Keep in mind that you are building up knowledge and a body consciousness along a definite path. So please don't invent other patterns while you are doing this work. Don't mix these exercises with others; don't even casually play with the objects that you juggle with. Later, after you have carefully developed your juggling ability, you can experiment with innovations. Try to follow these instructions as closely as you can. Each word comes out of practical experience with hundreds of students. If you stay right with me in these lessons, you will become a good juggler and you may learn a lot about yourself along the way.

If you have an enormous amount of trouble with Two Throws, I suggest that you alternate it with the One-Throw practice from the last lesson. You may just surprise yourself in an unguarded moment by breaking through into some new territory. Again, when you can stay in Home Position during the Two-Throw volley ten times in a row, go on to the next lesson.

Lesson 5: Three Throws

One problem about learning juggling, as well many other things, is that each time you add a piece on to what you already know, you run the risk of losing everything you have achieved so far. It's like a toy with odd-shaped pieces that you keep stacking up into a tower that gets shakier and shakier. In juggling, however, the crashing-down, if it happens to you at all, is only temporary. Although in the beginning you may find that the third throw upsets everything you've done, it will all will be restored to you later. Each piece that you add is like a rough-hewn block of stone that has to be shaped to fit in with the other stones already in place.

As preparation for this lesson do the Two-Throws Practice that you were working on in the last lesson. When you observe the very last part of the volley, you will see that you ended up by catching a ball in your right hand. The only new thing in this lesson will be to empty your right hand of the ball that is there just before catching the third ball. This last ball has not come into the discussion yet. It will be referred to as the third ball throughout this lesson. In the beginning, you may just throw it away in any direction to get rid of it. In a short time, you will be able to throw it to your left hand to complete the third throw. It should start out in the *palm* of your right hand before you begin the volley.

If you take everything I have said about the second throw and reverse the words "right" and "left," you will have the proper instructions for the third throw. In other words, you should throw the ball from your left hand (second throw) wide of your right hand, leaving plenty of room for the third ball to come from your right hand, to pass up under it, and to land in your left hand. You now have an Exchange taking place over your right hand as well as over your left. With Three Throws you will notice that each ball ends up in the opposite hand from the one it started in.

Now that you are throwing all three balls, you will be tempted to get them all up in the air as quickly as possible. In the previous lesson you may have had some difficulty waiting for the first ball to come down almost to your hand before throwing the second ball. Here, you must also wait for the second to almost land before throwing the third. Learn to wait—avoid reaching up for the ball. (You can check for this by freezing to see where your hands and arms are.) Once you get into juggling a little, you will see that it is actually a lot slower than it seemed at first. Just wait patiently for the ball, and it will eventually fall down into your hand.

Rhythm. If your rhythm is correct, and you

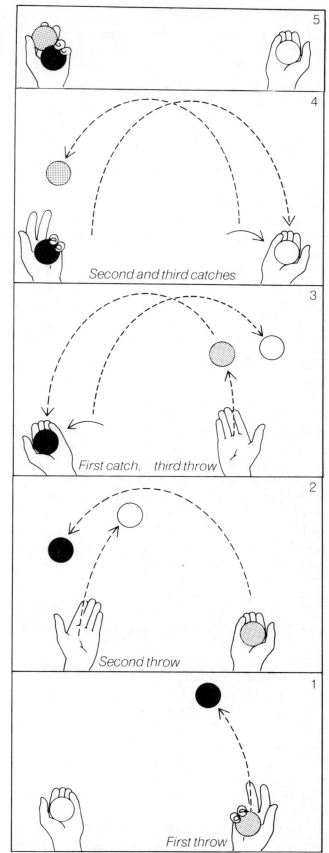

Second and third catches

First catch. third throw

Second throw

First throw

Three-Throws Practice. Alternate throws from right. left and right hands

are waiting for the ball on each catch, you should become aware of four evenly spaced beats: THROW • THROW • THROW • CATCH. The first two catches are very close to the second two throws, respectively, and are not shown. (This could be counted showing these two Exchanges as: THROW • EXCHANGE • EXCHANGE • CATCH.) If your rhythm pattern is more like: THROW • THROW • THROW . . . CATCH, then you are throwing the second and third balls too soon and not waiting long enough. If you do this, then after you get all three balls into the air you will find there is nothing more you can do until they start to come down. This is why there is a pause in the rhythm pattern. Of course, when they all do come down, you will have more balls to handle than you have hands available. Try to get these four beats exactly even, as the three beats were in the last lesson.

Full Egg-Beater. Notice that as you throw the second ball with your left hand, your hand comes up a little and continues to go around in a little circle. When you throw the third ball with your right hand, it makes the same kind of movement one beat later. Since your two hands come in toward the center at different times, the effect is something like an egg-beater with its blades intertwined. It's not exactly like that, since in juggling your hands never come into the central area or overlap each other. However, thinking of this egg-beater rhythm will help your hands make the right motions for Cascade juggling.

Self-Checking. In this lesson you are training your right hand to do the Exchange that your left hand learned to do in the previous lesson. Don't expect it to be any easier or to take less time. You will probably find that the third catch in your left hand will be way out in front of you somewhere. This may be because the first ball is thrown from your right hand and the third ball is later thrown from that same hand. Check by freezing. If you let the third ball roll forward in your hand onto your fingers before throwing it, it will already have a lot of forward motion. Once it gets on your fingers, you can no longer pop it properly, and it will inevitably roll from your fingers and spin around. This will make it go forward instead of up. Check

to see if you are doing this by watching the design on the ball.

Up to now the tasks you have been given to do constitute a kind of training. They should have become automatic by now. This has its advantages and disadvantages. The automatic habit is hard to break. What you should do is decide to let something become automatic while you still have ultimate control over it. The part of your juggling that you have already established can now go by itself, without your conscious intervention. This will leave you free to apply your full attention to new tasks or variations. In the course of these lessons, layer upon layer will be added to what has already become automatic. Each new skill is only preparation for another one more difficult, more advanced, but also more exciting, interesting and challenging. If you spend sufficient time on each step, it will all be easy. But if you try to go too fast, the steps will not be properly integrated, and you will end up having to devote your complete conscious attention to every small detail. Make sure you learn and practice each lesson really well before going on to the next.

Three-Throws Practice. Stand in Home Position. Place two balls in your right hand and one in your left. Throw the first ball from your right hand, sending it wide of your left hand over your left thumb. Throw the second ball from your left hand in under the incoming first ball, up and over and landing wide of your right hand. Before this second ball lands in your right hand, send the third ball up from your right hand, under the incoming ball, over and across to the left hand. Freeze on the last two catches.

As the practice gets more complex, it becomes increasingly important to freeze. From now on, Freezing will always be on the last two balls caught. Take a good look at everything. There are now many more chances for major errors. In juggling, errors tend to multiply, and you may be throwing some wild stuff by now. You have to tame each level before moving on. Check the spin on the balls to see if you are rolling them out of your hands or not. Make sure that you are always popping the balls.

One special note: In order to avoid handing the ball back to your right hand each time you start the next volley, you should *throw* it back to the other hand as a One Throw. This is to keep you from reinforcing the habit of putting your hands in front of your stomach. Practice by doing a Three Throw alternating with a One Throw from the left hand.

You may expect to spend as much time on this step as on the one before, if not longer. If you have trouble, either drop back temporarily to the previous step or alternate the Three-Throws Practice with the Two-Throws Practice. When you are doing this step perfectly ten times in a row, and you are satisfied with how it feels, go on to the next lesson.

Lesson 6: Four Throws

By this time, you have probably become aware of the general approach of the Carlo Method, and from now on I will be saying less and less on the details of how to work. Most of this has been said in the previous lessons, which you should review from time to time if you feel the need.

In this lesson, you will be throwing the ball that was sitting in your left hand when you caught the last of the three throws. This is the first ball you threw, and now you are going to throw it a second time. If you substitute a red ball for the very first ball thrown, you will see that this same ball is also the fourth throw. Four Throws is similar to what you were doing in the lesson on Two Throws, but comes two throws later. The main difference is that you have had two more throws during which to make errors. For this reason quite a bit of effort still is required.

If you have not already done so, you will soon see the repetitive nature of the Regular Cascade. Right now you have all you need to know in order to do three-ball juggling. All it requires is the execution of alternating left-hand and right-hand Exchanges. In other words, three-ball juggling consists of having a ball in each hand and one ball in the air. The direction toward which the ball in the air is moving indicates the hand over which the next

Exchange will take place.

Rhythm. As you start to do more throws, don't try to impose your rhythm on the balls. They have their own rhythm, which is actually determined by the height to which they are thrown. They are not like a machine that goes along in a strictly even rhythm. Nor is their rhythm exactly like music. Lost beats are not recoverable as they are in the dotted rhythms of music. Stay with the balls and watch them, and take your rhythm from what they are doing.

Planning. There is a temptation, once you see this pattern of repeated moves, to want to continue the volley indefinitely. Resist this temptation. In this phase of the work, and for some time to come, you should always decide beforehand exactly what you are going to do, and then set out to do it. Keep working until you achieve what you planned. This is the only way to proceed consciously. Until you are much more advanced and experienced, and ready to perform, always decide beforehand exactly how many throws you are going to do. No matter how well the volley seems to be going, stop when you have reached your planned limit. You control the balls; don't let them control you.

Drift. Another reason for this need to plan is the factor I call "Drift." You may decide to go on juggling when you find yourself doing fine for a while. All of a sudden you are moving forward after the balls, and then you are finally running. You are a victim of Drift. Actually, you weren't doing that well at all. The errors that you were making in the first two or three throws were too small to matter; you were able to cover for them. With the addition of more throws, especially throws that you haven't worked on, the errors start to accumulate until they are so huge that you are no longer able to rescue the situation. What will you have gained by running after these fleeing spheres?

One major cause of Drift is that as soon as you reach forward to catch a badly thrown ball, the next ball being thrown from that hand will be affected by the reaching and will also be thrown forward. Each time you move out to rescue a forward ball, you throw the next ball worse. This effect increases exponentially, Drift becomes inundation, and you have no choice but to run faster, like Alice, to keep up with the ever-receding balls.

One way to avoid or minimize Drift is to try to throw the ball in your hand exactly in the direction you want it to go, ignoring the catch completely. Then, split seconds later, move your empty hand out for the catch. Make sure that no anticipated motion from the catch gets into the throw that comes just before it. Another way to monitor Drift is to stand facing a wall, very close to it, so that you can gauge forward-and-back distance. In this way, when you throw a ball forward, it hits the wall and forces you to stop juggling.

Another way to avoid Drift is to observe your juggling using the Freeze. Do a fixed number of throws, and freeze on the last two catches. If you do this carefully, watching very closely, you will be able to spot any drifting before it gets unmanageable. If you start to drift, cut down your volley by one throw. If you were working on six throws at the time, cut it down to five for a while. In this case you might try alternating five throws with six to trick yourself into getting to the next higher level.

If you are having trouble with your right or left hand specifically, you might cut the volley by two throws. This means that you will still be ending the volley in the same hand. In this way, you can compare the Freeze after four throws, for example, with that after six, and look for differences. As you clear up difficulties, add throws back, one at a time. Always decide how many you are going to do, and do them. Then stop.

When you have increased the number of throws to ten or twelve, you may suddenly enter into a new phase where you become aware of the infinity of what you are doing. Somehow there is a ball up there that's never going to come down. You realize suddenly that you never have to stop; that you can juggle forever. A mysterious quality enters into what you are doing. In moments like these, and there will be many, all the struggle you have gone through will be forgotten.

Four-Throws Practice. Remember to return

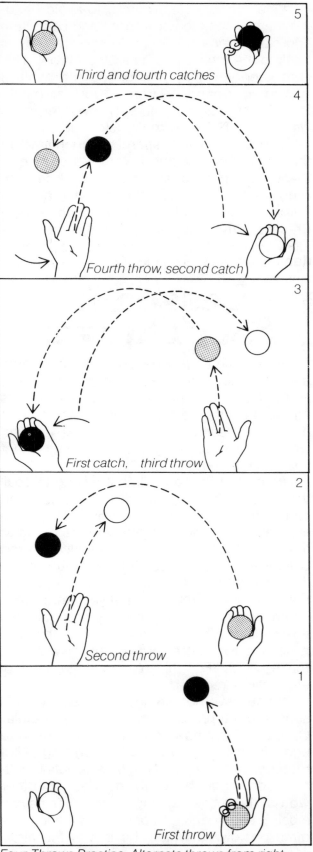

Four-Throws Practice. Alternate throws from right, left, right and left hands

to Home Position before starting each volley. Center yourself. Be aware of yourself, the room, the balls, the Tray Plane, and the Wall Plane. Relax. Don't let your body get into some tense position. Don't hold your breath while working. Don't work your mouth or hunch your shoulders. Always set a definite number of throws, do them, and stop, no matter how tempting it is to go on. As your needs dictate, change the number of throws up or down. Freeze on the last two catches. Check for stepping, body turn, and bent knees. Check elbow position to see if you are reaching or lifting your arms.

Many-Throws Practice. In the last five lessons you have been working through what is called the "Cascade Progression," a series of steps in which the number of throws is gradually increased, enabling you to sneak up on your goal. There are other progressions in this book that help you sneak up on other difficult areas.

In this Progression you will eventually reach a place where you can do an indefinite number of throws entirely without Drift or variation of any kind; a kind of "Look, Ma, I'm juggling" place. When you are really there, you should stop counting throws and start smoothing out your pattern. Up to now, if you have been doing it right, the Exchanges have been relatively late and short, resulting in a kind of choppy rhythm. You can get a smoother pattern by throwing the balls a little sooner, thus making the Exchanges longer. The next lesson will deal with solidifying and refining your work. Work on perfecting your present juggling by letting the volley go as long as possible, just to assure yourself that there is absolutely no Drift. When you are satisfied with your three-ball Cascade, go on to the next lesson.

II.
Variations
in
Ball
Juggling

Lesson 7: Solidifying Your Juggling

Before starting this lesson you should be able to sustain a volley indefinitely, absolutely without Drift. There will be many new things to learn in these advanced lessons. Aside from their value for their own sake, these new areas are designed to help solidify your Cascade work. Proceed carefully. If you jump ahead before the basic patterns are really learned, the work you do will confuse you and may actually destroy some of what you have already learned, making it doubly difficult for you to go on to new material. Even in this advanced section, each lesson is part of a carefully worked out plan. Each lesson prepares you for the next and assumes that you have worked through the previous one.

This lesson consists of sections I call Explorations. They give you some freedom insofar as how intensely you want to investigate them. You should make an attempt to do each one because some of them may be referred to later in the book.

SOME EXPLORATIONS FOR FUN

(1) Rhythm. Obtain some source of rhythmic sound, such as a metronome, a record, a song on the radio, or even a dripping water faucet; anything with a definite beat will serve the purpose. Try to juggle so that each hand does an Exchange (throw–catch) on a rhythmic beat. Use short, choppy Exchanges. This is contrary to some of the things I have just told you, but the only way you can get control over anything is to be able to do it in all possible ways. The height of the throws becomes very important here, but after a while you will be able to feel exactly what is needed. One way of adjusting the rhythm is to reach up for a ball to cut out a piece of time. I assume you understand that this reaching is for this specific purpose. It is conscious reaching, not an uncontrollable act.

Drumming. Stand at a table or a kitchen counter and juggle with your hands close to the surface. Then lower your juggling slowly until the backs of your hands or your knuckles are pounding on the table. This will help you hear the rhythm of your work, force your hands not to move up and down so much, and improve your catching and throwing.

(2) Half-Juggling. Although this is a partner rather than a solo technique, which rightly belongs among the lessons in that category, it is placed here because it is fairly easy and can be helpful to you at this moment in your development. This would be a good time to find a partner, someone with whom you work well and who has roughly the same level of skill as yourself. There will be much that you can do together later in the work. Half-Juggling is defined as two half-jugglers (half-wits?) working together to make one full juggler.

Side-By-Side. Stand to your partner's left. Put your right arm behind your back and forget about it. Your partner puts his left arm behind his back in the same way. This leaves your left arm and your partner's right arm free to juggle. With these two hands the two of you can do just about any variation that a single person can do alone. Your partner will start with two balls in his right hand, since he is on the right side. You will have one ball in your left hand. Stand very close to each other to make the distance between your hands about the same as the distance between your own shoulders. If you and your partner happen to be particularly friendly, you could put your unused arms around each other.

Side-by-Side is especially useful in teaching juggling to a beginning student, since he can concentrate on one hand at a time. He does not have to be aware of the whole thing at once. Even two beginners can help each other greatly through this Side-by-Side work. That is one reason it is given here. Make sure that you and your partner work on both the right and left sides. As you work you will be gradually tuning in on each other while you get used to the rhythm of the other person, something which is vital to all partner work.

Face-To-Face. Here you and your partner face each other and put your left arms behind your backs. Use your right hands for making diagonal or corner throws to each other. If you stand close to one another, you can throw the balls directly across from one side to the other, using the same general direction as in solo juggling. This is closely related to Take-Aways, to be covered in a later lesson.

(3) Eye-Independence Exercises. The following exercises are designed to help your juggling become independent from your direct vision. This will train your arms and hands to carry on the juggling so that more of your attention is available for other things.

Mirror. Stand in front of a full-length mirror, if you have one, or any large mirror. Watch your image in the mirror as you juggle. This will help you get your eyes away from your pattern, a necessary step before really feeling at home with what you are doing. The only problem you may have to deal with here is the fact that reaching forward for the ball in real space is reaching the other way in terms of the mirror. As you watch yourself juggle, slowly turn sideways, continuing as far as you can, until you are watching yourself almost over your shoulder. Throw the balls higher so that you can continue to see them.

This mirror practice is especially useful when you begin working toward performing for an audience. You can check to see if you are making faces, letting your mouth hang open, or blocking the view of your face by throwing in front of it. There is nothing worse than having pictures taken and seeing when they are developed that every one has some unidentified flying object smack in the middle of your face.

Squint and Blind. Practice squinting while you are juggling. This is another way for you to get more control of your hands. As you close your eyes completely, you will be doing blind juggling, something that has not been thoroughly explored. I have been able to make about seven catches with my eyes closed. It would be interesting to know the maximum number of catches that can be made blindfolded. Don't squint for long periods of time; give your eyes a rest. Another technique is to attempt to juggle in a darkened room with just a little light from a candle or a stick of incense.

Shadow Juggling. Juggle watching your shadow rather than the balls themselves. You will need some small source of light, such as a single bright light bulb or rays from the sun, to produce good sharp shadows. It will take you a little time to figure out which ball makes which shadow. Experiment by turning your body at various angles to the light. If you juggle indoors with a number of different spotlights on the balls, you will be able to make some interesting patterns on the floor and walls, which you can watch instead of the balls.

Glance. Let your glance travel away from the balls. First, focus your vision *through* the balls to the wall or floor beyond them. Then let your glance start to wander upward and around the room in various directions. You may see just the very tops of the arcs of the balls in your peripheral vision. This is enough to juggle with. After you get good at this, you should be able to read aloud from a newspaper while juggling, crack jokes with the people watching you, or carry on a conversation while looking at another person and making all the necessary facial gestures, nods, and signs of recognition and understanding.

Pattern Size. Your juggling pattern has a certain size. You can think of it as a picture frame sitting in your hands. In the work until now, you have been standing in Home Position, with your hands and arms shoulder-distance apart, and throwing the balls up to about the level of your eyes. This defines the width and height of your juggling pattern. Now that this pattern has been well established through long, hard work, you can begin to modify these basic factors of width and height to produce patterns of other sizes. There are nine basic variations in pattern size, and all are possible combinations of Width (Narrow, Medium, and Wide) and Height (Low, Medium, and High). Let's take a look at these. They will be presented roughly in the order of difficulty and numbered from one to nine.

(1) Medium Pattern. The juggling pattern that you have been doing is "Medium Width, Medium Height." In the discussion that follows, this will be referred to as the Medium Pattern.

(2) High Pattern. After Medium Pattern, the easiest thing to do is the High Pattern. Your hands remain in Home Position, but the balls are thrown higher. This does not mean that you suddenly throw all the balls up to the ceiling. Instead, you should practice the Medium Pattern until it becomes stable. Then very slowly increase the height of the throws. The rhythm will slow down because it takes longer for the balls to go up and come down. Don't lose the evenness of the rhythm. If you miss, go back to Medium Pattern and work into it again. Avoid having your arms fly around too much. There is a great temptation here to do this, since you will have to throw the balls higher. Try to keep as much energy as possible in your hands. When you get the pattern up to about three feet over your head, you can slowly bring it down again. Do not break the continuity. You should always continue to juggle while returning to Medium Pattern from any variation. Work on this until you can go from Medium to High and back to Medium Pattern in a single volley.

(3) Low Pattern. Another variation you can do while your hands are in Home Position is the Low Pattern. Here you will find that the rhythm speeds up, and this will be a real test of your ability. If you are juggling efficiently, using minimum energy in your throws and catches (no Wind-up and no Follow-through), you won't have any trouble. If you find that you don't have enough time to make the throws and catches, go back and review the previous lessons. Remember that you need only cradle the ball, not clutch it. If you do this, you will need much less time to get the ball in and out of your hand.

Smoothing and Lowering. Until now, I have given you a definite kind of *marcato* beat for your rhythm. Marcato is a musical term meaning marked time. Each popping of the ball is a definite beat, like the beat an orchestra conductor might make with his baton. This sharp, choppy wait-and-throw rhythm has served a good purpose—it has helped you define and to deliver the energy you needed to the proper hand at the proper time. It also helped you to divide what you were doing into pieces and was an aid to counting throws.

As you juggle lower, however, you will find that you won't have any time to make this beat so definite. The marcato rhythm has served its purpose and can be shelved. Just let those definite beats begin to smooth themselves out. Keep the popping and the energy in the hands, but let more energy flow in what you are doing. Try to keep your hands moving in little continuous circles. The inner orchestra conductor is now leading a legato passage, a violin melody without beats. You should be getting your pattern lower and lower in this exercise, injecting a smoothness into all your work. From now on, it is better to use a lower pattern so you can see over the balls. You will find that this smoother way of juggling will be a great help. To practice, start with Medium Pattern, go to Low Pattern, and back to Medium all in one volley.

(4) Narrow Pattern. The next pattern in order of difficulty is the Narrow Pattern. Bring your hands close together in front of you. Juggle the balls at normal height but so that they go up and down in a narrow column, almost touching as they go past one another. Notice that for the first time you are not in Home Position. Be sure you return to Home Position when you resume Medium Pattern.

(5) Narrow High Pattern. From the pattern above you can easily extend your juggling vertically into Narrow-High Pattern. See instructions for the High Pattern.

(6) Narrow-Low Pattern. You can also easily go to low juggling. It is possible to juggle so narrow and so low that the balls almost touch and actually appear to be rolling over each other. This is a nice goal for this area of work. Now do steps 4, 5, and 6 together as a unit. Do only narrow juggling, starting with Medium, going to High, back to Medium, to Low, and back again to Medium, all during a single volley. In all variations you should always be able to recover the Medium Pattern with ease.

(7) Wide Pattern. The hardest patterns— the Wide Patterns—have been left till last. These are harder because your hands are wide apart, and you don't have much freedom of action to go after any wrongly thrown balls. Also, especially in Wide-Low work, it is much more difficult to catch a ball that is going hori-

zontally rather than vertically. You will find it easier if you rotate your hands toward each other. (This is why when jugglers are working in the same room and one picks up another's dropped ball, he will throw it high rather than straight across, so that it comes down vertically and is easier to catch. This is one of the courtesies observed by professional jugglers.)

In the beginning, start with the Medium Pattern you know and slowly start to widen your hands from Home Position. Aim for a continuous volley, from Medium to Wide and back to the Medium Pattern.

(8) Wide-Low Pattern. After you have become accustomed to this wider juggling, start dropping the height slowly. Make sure that you use fairly heavy balls, because one slight error will send very light balls flying. After a while the height can go down as low as four or five inches, or even lower. It is also possible to make the balls look as though they were passing through each other.

(9) Wide-High Pattern. The most difficult pattern is the Wide-High. Not only are your hands quite wide apart, but you have to throw the balls much further, and so you need a little more vertical motion in your hands to do this. Also, the balls are tracing huge curved arcs that have to be exactly right. It is very easy for even an experienced juggler to miss while doing a Wide-High Pattern.

Pattern-Size Practice. Stand in Home Position. Do the Medium Pattern. Then go to High, down to Low, and back to Medium Pattern. While still juggling, bring your hands close together and do the Narrow Patterns: Medium, High, Low, and Medium again. Then widen your hands slowly to do Medium Wide, Low, and High, and back to Medium Wide. Stop when you return to your normal pattern. If you can do all this on a single volley, you are ready to move on.

Mixed Throws. Another area you can work on, after mastering each of the patterns, is "Mixed Throws." Throw some High, some Low, some Wide, and some Narrow. This randomness is not because you *have* to juggle this way; it is to show you that you are in control of your juggling and that you can *choose* to juggle this way.

After you have finished this work, you can truly call yourself a juggler. But don't be satisfied with this level of achievement—there are layers upon layers of deeper and more rewarding adventures in the lessons ahead, and after that, in the areas of your own investigation and experimentation.

Lesson 8: Body Positions

So far you have been working in a normal standing position. Now you are ready to experiment with some other positions. This will add interest and challenge to your juggling, and it will help further solidify what you already have learned. This will also help you keep your energy strictly in your hands, as you place your body in a variety of positions.

Standing. Before going on to other positions, there are a few things you can do while still standing. The simplest is to stand on one leg while juggling. If you have not yet stabilized your center completely, and if you move around a bit to continue your volley, this will help point out what you need to work on and root you to one spot. Another good exercise is to balance a book on your head while juggling. Doing this will immediately tell you a lot about any involuntary head and neck movements you are making, of which you might not have been aware. These simple exercises place a constraint on your work and therefore sharpen it.

Sitting. The easiest of the other positions is sitting. Don't sit on a low couch because your knees will come up into your face and get in the way of the balls. Choose some higher place, such as a straight-backed chair, a bar stool, or one arm of a sturdy couch. Sit straddling one corner, so that each leg can dangle at a low angle and be out of the way. With your legs out of the way, you will be able to juggle with very little trouble. As you work in this position, you will quickly discover just how much the rest of your body has been getting in on the act. Sitting forces the lower half of your body and much of the upper half to remain still, and it helps you to isolate and control your movement and bring it into your hands where it belongs. By resting your elbows on your knees or legs, you can keep your arms and hands from flailing. Sitting helps you to be more precise and careful in your juggling, and it prevents you from running after the balls.

Kneeling. Another very easy position is kneeling. Kneel on a pillow on the floor. Kneeling is especially useful if your room has a low ceiling or if you want to throw the balls quite high. Like sitting, kneeling also keeps you from running after the balls. And it has one decided advantage—it puts you close to the floor so that you easily can pick up dropped balls.

On the Floor. Sit on the floor, either against the wall or out in the middle of the room, and juggle with your hands in the same position as when you were standing. Sit cross-legged, or if you prefer, with your legs out in front of you. This is not a terribly comfortable position for many people, but it will test your juggling ability to the utmost. Try especially to stretch out your legs close together in front of you, and do the Wide Pattern. You can also place the backs of your hands almost on the floor next to your legs. While you are juggling in this position, slowly lean back so that you are lying or almost lying on the floor. The fully prone position is very difficult because the position of the hands in relation to the balls is very awkward. But this position is certainly worth a try.

On Your Back. Another difficult variation is lying on your back and juggling with your hands right up over your face, pushing the balls up from below. There are a lot of obstacles to this technique. For one thing, you will find it difficult to retrieve any balls that get too far away from you, since you will have to get up and fetch them each time. You might want to have an assistant to help you, or a very large collection of balls. One other possibility is to arrange some kind of sloping net all around you so that the balls always roll back to you, no matter where you throw them.

Another problem is that you are likely to be bopped in the face repeatedly by the falling balls until you learn to throw them so they will miss your face. The throw is very hard to get used to in the beginning. Use the Cascade Progression to explore this on-the-back juggling. Start with one ball and increase the number of throws slowly, going through all the levels outlined in the first lessons. You may have to put out a lot of effort, but I assure you it will be well worth it.

An alternative position to this one, using a similar throw, is to stand and lean way back so that you face straight up toward the ceiling. Juggle, pushing the balls upward, as you did lying on your back on the floor.

Body-Positions Practice. Stand in Home Position. Get a good steady juggling pattern going. Then slowly bend your knees, keeping your back as straight as possible. Lower yourself down onto one knee. Then let the other knee come down. Continue to drop down until you are sitting on your heels. Slowly lean over to one side and slide one leg out from under you. Then lean the other way and slide out your other leg. You will now be sitting on the floor with your legs stretched out in front of you. Try leaning back as far as you can without missing. Then reverse the whole process until you are standing again. The aim is to do this whole sequence without missing.

If you have an enormous amount of trouble with this, just go down a little way before returning to a standing position again. For instance, go down on one knee and come back up while still juggling. Later on, you will be able to extend it further.

Body Movements. Once you have your Cascade juggling absolutely solid, you can do just about anything you want with the rest of your body. This includes walking, running, turning, dancing, skipping, or jumping. You can move on level ground, step up onto objects or down from them, or go up or down stairs. Dancing to almost any kind of music while you are juggling gives you good training in handling rhythm, body position, energies, and centering, all at the same time. Juggling while skating or skiing is also worth investigating.

Contrivances. Various machines and gadgets are also fun to try.

(1) Rolling Cylinder. This is a well-known training device for circus performers and skiers. Juggling actually makes it easier to balance on a rolling cylinder, since the balls act like a gyroscope, defining a balance point and a body center for you. For safety, always keep your feet at the very ends of the board.

(2) Rolling Globe. This is a hard item to come by, since you can't buy at your local toy store a two-foot-diameter globe that is hard enough to stand on. You have to make one yourself. Only work with this globe when you have at least two other people to catch you if you fall; it is very dangerous. For bears it is simple, but not for people.

(3) Tight and Slack Wire. The best way to do this is to start with a board on edge, nailed to something. First use a wide board, later a narrow one, then the slack wire, and finally the tight one. (Without special equipment, it is almost impossible to get a wire tight enough.)

With any of these devices, juggling helps you to maintain your balance.

(4) Vehicles. Try juggling in a moving bus, train, or subway. Watch what the balls do as the vehicle speeds up or slows down. It's as if gravity were shifting around under your feet, which is quite an interesting sensation. The same effect can be seen if you juggle while you are walking, or running.

(5) Cycles. If you can ride a bicycle "no-handy," or if you are one of the few people who can ride a unicycle, the addition of juggling will be quite an accomplishment and is a fine practice for coordination of the whole body.

(6) Stilts. If you fasten stilts to your legs, so your hands are free, you will be able to juggle. How you are going to pick up a dropped ball? I can't tell you.

(7) Trapeze. One very advanced technique involves hanging by your legs from a properly constructed circus trapeze. Arch your body up forward and do the On-the-Back juggling described earlier. Arch your body the other way, toward your back, and do normal Cascade juggling. This is, I suppose, just about as far as you can go with this sort of thing.

Lesson 9: Reverse Cascade

Before you attempt to learn the Reverse Cascade, you should be really good at the Regular Cascade and have worked through the last few lessons carefully. You are going to be doing a lot of things differently now, and what you have already learned should be stored away carefully so that you don't lose it.

Underthrow and Overthrow. When you learned the Regular Cascade you were told to throw the ball up *under* the incoming ball. This produces the Cascade effect of balls going up in the middle and coming down on the outside. This basic throwing-under movement is called an "Underthrow." In this lesson you are going to learn to do just the reverse, that is, throwing the ball up *over* the incoming ball, which is an "Overthrow."

Tray-Plane Points. Recall the Tray Plane. In this plan, visualize four points, two close together on the left and two on the right. These points are named according to their location: Left-Outside, Left-Inside, Right-Inside, and Right-Outside. They mark where your hands are at various moments of throwing and catching. In the Regular Cascade, your right hand throws from the Right-Inside point. That ball then comes down at the Left-Outside point. Your left hand scoops it around to the Left-Inside point, where it is thrown back to the Right-Outside point. These Cascade

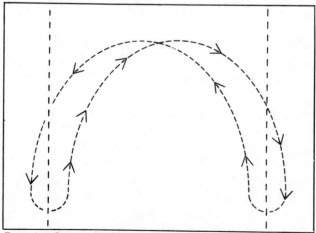

Regular Cascade. Balls go up in the middle and down on the sides

throws, starting from the Inside points on each side, are the Underthrows. When you were told earlier to throw wide at all costs, it was to make sure that you threw the ball all the way to the opposite Outside point.

Half-Reverse Cascade. Before you can learn the Full-Reverse Cascade, you must learn the Half-Reverse Cascade on each side. Let's start with the Half-Reverse on the right side. Here, your left hand does almost the same thing it did in the Regular Cascade. Your right hand will now be throwing from the Right-Outside point, instead of from the Inside point, thus making it an Overthrow. The incoming ball will be caught at the Right-Inside point, instead of the Outside. This means that your right hand in throwing goes up on the Outside now, and then as it catches, it comes down on the Inside. This is the exact reverse of the circular motion you did in the Regular Cascade. It will now be a counterclockwise motion—a Half Egg-Beater in reverse.

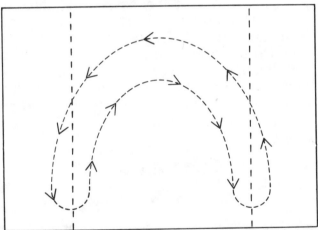

Half Reverse Cascade or Double Shower. Balls do not cross paths

Set-Up. If your right hand is going to be catching the ball at the Right-Inside point, it follows that your left hand is going to have to throw it there. This Inside point is nearer to your left hand, and so the ball is thrown from your left hand a shorter distance. The "Set-Up" is defined as *the throw before any given throw.* In order to give your right hand room to make an Overthrow, you should throw the Set-Up *short* from your left hand.

It also follows that since your right hand is now throwing from the Right-Outside point,

its throws will have to be longer than in the Regular Cascade in order to cover the greater distance between the points. To summarize: The Set-Up before an Overthrow must be *short;* the Overthrow itself must be *long.*

Half-Reverse Practice. Get three balls of different colors—say, red, green, and blue. Do a Regular Cascade. Each time the red ball comes around to the right hand, throw it as an Overthrow. By looking at the colors, you can work out just which ball will be the Set-Up. For instance, if you place the red ball in your right hand as the first one to be thrown, the Set-Up will be the other ball that started in that hand. It is essential that the Set-Up before any Overthrow always be short. If you don't throw the Set-Up short, you will have enormous difficulty finding room to make the next throw properly, and you will have a lot of mid-air collisions.

Notice as you work that the red ball comes around and is thrown as every third throw of your right hand. In between, the other two balls will be given regular Underthrows. Now advance to a rhythm of throwing *every other* ball from your right hand as an Overthrow. When you can do this, work on giving *every* ball coming from your right hand an Overthrow. For these last two exercises, it would probably be less confusing to go back to using balls of the same color. Throwing all the balls from one hand in any special way, such as an Overthrow, is called "Half-Showering." Half-Showering Overthrows in your right hand give you a Half-Reverse Cascade.

Now start again, and go through all this with your left hand. Do this until you can throw every ball from your left hand as an Overthrow. This will mean short Set-Ups from your right hand, and long throws from your left. If you are right-handed, you will find this completely contrary to your right-handed nature; but with enough concentration you will get it.

Tennis Variation. After you can do some Overthrows from each side, you should try the "Tennis Variation," which will help you move on to the Full-Reverse Cascade. Take a red ball and give it an Overthrow with your right hand. Then give that same ball an Overthrow back with your left hand. The red ball will appear to be floating over the other two. It looks a little like a tennis ball going back and forth over a net. The other two balls will be doing a kind of leapfrog thing down below. (This lower pattern is called "Vamping," and will be covered later.)

At first, pick the red ball and do an Overthrow from your right hand, return it with your left, and go back into Regular Cascade. Later, try for a longer run of Overthrows in both directions. One reason for this variation is to trick your left hand into learning how to do Overthrows. With your right hand doing one immediately before, it becomes easier for your left hand to do it through a kind of sympathetic vibration. Try it. The "Tennis" ball should be red and the other two dark, so that you heighten the contrast between the two things happening. Another way to emphasize the Tennis ball is to throw it from a higher point on one side to that point on the other, while keeping the other two Vamping balls as low as possible. This gives the feeling that you are doing two independent kinds of juggling at the same time.

Full-Reverse Cascade. To do the Full-Reverse you have to combine throwing everything that comes to each hand (called a "Full Shower"), which you did with one hand in the Half-Reverse, and the idea of throwing Overthrows alternately from both sides in Quick Succession, which you just did in the Tennis Variation. One difference here is that when

you are throwing everything from both sides as Overthrows, the catches will all be at the Inside points, and so the throws will not be quite as long. Notice that in the Full-Reverse Cascade your hands are making a reverse Egg-Beater; both are moving down in the middle and going up on the outside. Once you have this Overthrow juggling well in hand, combine it with variations in pattern size and body position.

Same-Hand Throw. In addition to the Underthrow and Overthrow, there is the "Same-Hand Throw." It is thrown as an Overthrow, with the same reverse rotation of the hand, but it does not go across to your left hand. It is thrown straight up in the air from your right hand, and it comes down into that hand again, landing on the outside, just like catching in the Regular Cascade. As it comes down, pop the next ball across to your left hand, and resume regular juggling. The effect of this is to delay the juggling by one throw; it will also reverse the order of the balls being thrown. Check by using balls of three different colors. You can also try a Same-Hand Tennis Variation. Do a Same-Hand Throw on each side alternately so that only one ball goes back and forth between your hands. Each of the other two balls stays in the hand it started in, just going up and down.

Lesson 10: Clawing

The "Claw" is an interesting variation on the ordinary way of catching and throwing a ball. Your hand quickly swoops down over the ball and grabs it from above, palm facing down. In order to do this easily, use lacrosse balls, baseballs, or other heavy balls. A heavy ball will stay around longer and will not fly away from your hand. The weight helps your hand to close around the ball as it hits your palm. Also, if you grab it just right and put some force behind it, a lacrosse ball makes a nice, smacking sound.

Catching. In the beginning you should use two white balls and one red one. Every time the red ball comes around to your right hand,

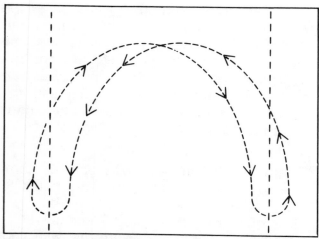

Full Reverse Cascade. Balls go up on the outside and come down in the middle

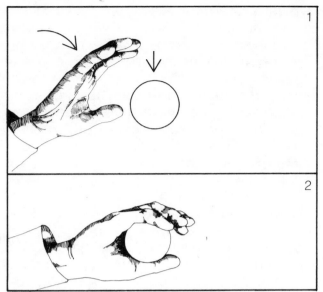

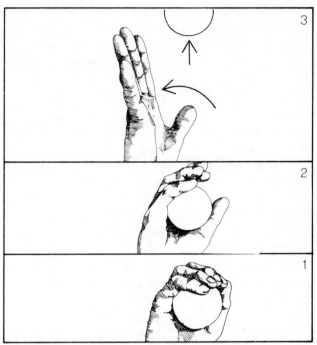

Clawing. Hand overtakes the ball as it falls

Throwing. Hand releases the ball as it rises

claw it as just described, and immediately turn your hand right-side-up to throw it again. To start, throw the ball to be clawed higher than normal, and then claw it at the top of its arc when it's stationary. In this position, your hand won't be palm-down so much as palm-forward. The higher throw gives you more time to grab the ball and bring it down. As you improve, you won't have to throw the balls quite so high, and you will be able to claw them after they have started to fall. This will speed up the juggling and the clawing effect. Finally, you will be able to Claw almost at the Tray Plane.

Throwing. While you are working on this catching technique, you should be learning how to throw the ball from your hand while it is still palm-down. The main problem is to judge at what exact moment you should open your hand in order to get the ball to a certain height. When you first try it, the balls will probably go to all different heights. Later, you will be able to achieve more control. The advantage of keeping your hand palm-down to throw is that you will have more time to throw and catch if you are not continually turning your hand over in between throwing and catching.

Full-Shower Progression. As with the Overthrows in the last lesson, you should gradually develop toward doing a Full Shower of Clawing. You will recall that a Full Shower

refers to doing the same special throw or catch every time in both hands. The "Full-Shower Progression" is a series of carefully graded steps that will help you sneak up on your goal. I gave you most of the steps informally in the lesson describing Overthrows, but here they will be given in a more detailed and systematized way, so that they can be used for general application. The Full-Shower Progression consists of the following:

1. Right Hand, Occasional — Every few times the red ball comes around, it is thrown in the special way (Clawing, for instance).
2. Right Hand, Every Third — Every time the *red* ball comes around, which is the same as every third ball of any kind.
3. Right Hand, Every Other — Alternate right-hand throws.
4. Right Hand, Shower — Every throw in the right hand; really a Half-Shower or a Slow Succession.
5. Tennis-type Throw — Special throw given with the same ball as it reaches each hand.
6. Two in Quick Succession (Two in a Row) — Like step 5, except that you claw the very next ball in the left hand, one ball sooner than in step 5 (right-left).
7. Left Hand, Occasional — See step 1.

8. Left Hand, Every Third — See Step 2.
9. Left Hand, Every Other — See step 3.
10. Left Hand, Shower — See step 4.
11. Three in Quick Succession (Three in a Row). — Right, left, right.
12. Full-Shower (Many in Quick Succession or Many in a Row). — Right, left, right, left, etc.; increase the numbers of throws slowly.

The Full-Shower Progression will be used several times in this book. The idea is to train your right or better hand first. (If you are left-handed, reverse the hands in the list of steps.) Then bridge across to your weaker hand by doing successive Tennis throws in both hands. The mechanism is called "Transference"; it means that your left hand will be able to do something better if your right hand has just done it a second before. When you have trained your left hand to work on its own until it can do a Half-Shower, the Quick Succession (right, left, right) will help you to feel the timing and the rhythm as you go from right to left and from left to right. This also sets the groundwork for a Full Shower, a continuous run of Quick Succession right-left-right-lefts, which is the objective of the whole Progression. As you work, you should try to keep your palms down all the time. This helps create the effect of the balls disappearing and reappearing in your hands.

Be very careful with Full-Shower Clawing. This variation is a very high-energy thing. Don't tense up; don't hold your breath. Don't let the energy build up so you can't come back to the Regular Cascade when you want to. Stay in control at all times. Juggling is not the thing to do when you want to go off dreaming somewhere. If you miss a ball, or catch it just on your fingertips without being able to keep hold of it, it will without doubt fly across the room like a cannon ball, with possibly disastrous results.

Over-the-Head. From Full-Shower Clawing, you can slowly start throwing and catching the balls higher and higher, finally getting them up over your head. There is a strong tendency for the balls to continue to go back over your head and come down behind you, out of your reach. Therefore, be on guard.

Upward Clawing. After you are quite well along with the Downward Clawing you have been doing, you should try Upward Clawing. This means that as the ball is falling into your hand (palm-up now), you wait as long as you can, and then suddenly claw upward on the ball, releasing the one that you have in your hand. This is the equivalent of an extremely fast, late, and short Exchange, perhaps only three or four inches long. The ball that you release has a lot of energy behind it, and will go quite high in the air.

While you are waiting for this ball to come down again, you have time to do anything you like. You can let your other hand with its ball fly up to the same height, and let it come down as the free ball comes down, so the ball and the other hand and ball are going up and down together. It's hard to visualize, but the effect of this is wildly hypnotic.

Sideways Clawing. When you get really advanced and have a safe place to work (not for you, but for the furniture), try the "Sideways Claw." There are two variations of this, the "Inward Claw" and the "Outward Claw." The Outward variation is much easier. With your right hand, start by clawing the red ball straight outward to the right. After a while, do two in a row with your right hand. As you claw the second ball, you will see that the release of the first ball will send it low, straight across to your left hand. If you succeed in doing a Full-Shower of Sideways Clawing, all anyone will see is a blur between your two hands as the balls become visible one at a time. If you can do more than six throws before missing, you will really have achieved something. As in all advanced work, recovery is very important. It is all well and good to do far-out variations, but you must be able to return to the Regular Cascade before you miss. When you miss, you take all the energy out of the fine work that you created during the volley. The only way out is to have someone photograph you just before you miss.

Single-Wide Claw. Juggle using a narrow pattern. Then send one ball very low and very fast out to your right side. Then reach way out and claw this ball very fast, about a foot or more to the right of your pattern. If this is a red ball, you can create the feeling that the ball, by the special way it behaves, has a personality all its own. Many of the variations you have already seen and many to come are adaptable to such imaginative treatment.

Clawing Practice. Work on catching and later throwing with the Claw. Then work through the Full-Shower Progression, making sure that you give your weaker hand the attention it needs. Once you can do Shower Clawing, work on Upward and Sideways Clawing. Over-the-Head Clawing is more advanced. The Single-Wide Claw is especially good for performing.

Lesson 11: Body Throws

Once your Regular Cascade has become really stable and goes by itself totally without conscious effort, you will be ready to develop the various "Body Throws." A Body Throw simply means a special throw with relation to some part of the body. Each type of throw will be taken up in turn. One characteristic of all Body Throws is that they require more time to execute than regular throws. The only way to obtain the extra time needed is to make the Set-Up, or throw before the Body Throw, a little higher than normal. This will delay its coming down and give you time to do the required moving around. You need time to get your hand out to the place where you will make the Body Throw, such as behind your back, and time to bring it back to Home Position to catch the incoming Set-Up throw.

Behind-the-Back Throw. This is the easiest of the Body Throws. Swing your right arm down past your hip and then have it come up behind and very close to your back. Let go of the ball, which will continue up over your left shoulder and into your left hand. Keeping your arm close to your back will prevent the ball from going too far forward. Do not lean over forward, since this will add a forward motion to the ball and put it out of your reach.

As you continue to work on this, avoid moving your body as much as possible. Make your arms do the work. Consistency is important here; you should work toward placing every Behind-the-Back Throw directly into your left hand as it sits in Home Position. First, practice individual, isolated throws without juggling. Next, begin your volley with such a throw. Finally, incorporate this throw in the *middle* of a volley. The Freeze is useful here to help place your throw accurately.

Shoulder Throw. Once you get your hand behind your back, there is another direction in which you can throw the ball. You have just thrown the ball to your opposite shoulder. Now you will be throwing the ball to your same shoulder. Extend your elbow straight out to the right. Your right hand will be under your upper arm as you throw the ball. The ball will come up over your upper arm or shoulder into your right hand. This is one of the Same-Hand Throws. As before, try to place the ball in your right hand when your hand is in Home Position.

Both of these are high throws. Avoid throwing the following ball from the opposite hand too soon; wait until the high throw is almost down. With practice you will be able to roll the ball up over your shoulder and not interrupt the timing of the juggling at all.

Under-the-Leg Throw. As you do an "Under-the-Leg Throw," pay special attention to the movement of your leg and to the fact that you are throwing from a lower point than normal. If you have trouble doing this, break the movement up into pieces: Practice bringing your right or left leg up very quickly without losing your balance, or practice stooping over or crouching as you juggle. Again, start with individual throws, and only later work them into your juggling. The important things here are consistency in placing the ball, economy of movement, and recovery of your Regular Cascade.

The two types of Leg Throws are the "Near-Leg" and "Far-Leg Throws." Your right hand will throw under your right or Near Leg, or it can throw under your left or Far Leg. The Far-Leg Throw is the easier and more natural of the two. Of course, give your left hand a workout, too.

There are two additional Leg Throws that fall into the category of advanced variations, but I will discuss them briefly here.

Forward-Center Leg Throw. This is a special near-leg throw. Stand with your legs apart and throw the ball through from behind as you lean back. Don't lift your legs during this throw.

Backward-Center Leg Throw. Bend forward and throw the ball through your legs so that it comes up behind you. As you straighten up it will come forward over your head or shoulder. Catch it and continue juggling.

Both of these special leg throws are quite difficult. They severely limit your time because they are done while a ball is in the air. You must throw extremely accurately, move your body rapidly, and not get dizzy or confused. Again, work with an individual throw before incorporating it into your juggling.

Under-the-Leg Catches. Normally, your hand returns to Home Position to make the catch that follows these special throws. With the Under-the-Leg variations, if you throw the ball to the point where you make the special throw, you can also catch it there. It's as if you had moved your whole operation away from Home Position to this new location under your leg. The Statue of Liberty variation, to be discussed later, also uses this relocation of Home Position.

Under-the-Wrist Throw. A third group of Body Throws involves your wrist, hand, and arm. In the "Under-the-Wrist Throw," your right hand goes across under your left wrist and throws its ball straight up to the left of your left hand. Your right hand then goes quickly back and catches the next ball in its normal spot in Home Position. Your left hand then catches the ball coming down to it on the outside (the special throw), and from that point you go back into the Regular Cascade. The only variation for your left hand is that the special throw comes in from the left side of it. Avoid the tendency to pull in your left arm to make room for the special throw. Build up these throws to a Full Shower.

Crossed-Wrists Juggling. Place the balls in your hands as for the Regular Cascade. Then cross your forearms at the wrists

and juggle in that position without uncrossing them. You don't have much wrist action available, and so this is a good exercise for strengthening your wrists. You will find that your crossed arms will move around as a unit, something like a child's imitation of the motion of a plane.

If you uncross your wrists while you are juggling this way, you will automatically go back into the Regular Cascade. One hand or the other will spontaneously execute a kind of Same-Hand Throw, although the ball will actually go to the other hand. This change of variation is easy because you are going toward a familiar juggling pattern.

It is somewhat harder to go from the Regular Cascade back to the Crossed Wrists while juggling. Start to make a Same-Hand Throw with your right hand, throwing the ball to the outside of that hand. At the same time, bring your left hand in under your right hand, cross your wrists, and catch that Same-Hand Throw. From this position your left hand throws its ball and you are back into Crossed-Wrists juggling. You must use this type of Same-Hand throw to make the change. Eventually you will be able to go back and forth between these two patterns at will.

Statue of Liberty Throw. Begin with the Regular Cascade. Then slowly raise your right hand and arm out of Home Position. Go as high as you can with it. You will find that almost without effort, your left hand will be throwing the balls higher and higher to get them up to your right hand. Also, your right hand will begin more and more to drop the balls back into your left hand. This is an easy variation that can be made to look impressive. You can get into a position where your right arm is fully raised up and forward and your left arm is down behind you, similar to a ballet position. There are many other possibilities of this type, which are waiting to be developed by the right person.

Body-Throws Practice. With each of the Body Throws, except the Crossed-Wrists, Center-Leg, and Statue of Liberty, you can use a red ball as a marker that will help you build up to a Full-Shower Progression. If you have trouble at first, you can begin by throwing the red ball every third or every other time, giving you plenty of time to recover. A Full Shower of Under-the-Wrist throws is quite easy, especially when compared to a Full Shower of Behind-the-Back throws, which amounts to doing all the juggling behind your back as though you were facing the other way. A Full Shower of Under-the-Leg throws will keep your arms and legs as busy as a bug on its back.

Body Catches. Body catches are good ways to end your volley, since they are catches without accompanying throws. They are all in the realm of advanced work. Any place on your body where you can hold a ball can provide for a possible body catch. Try bending over so that a ball can land on your back (keep your arms up so that your shoulder blades form a little cup for the ball, which is not terribly difficult); catching the ball under your chin (it can be dropped or plucked back into your juggling); or catching the ball between your chin and your shoulder (like the old apple game). More exotic catches employ the armpit, elbow, knee joint, between the thigh and the stomach with your leg raised, and between your legs, knees, and elbows. I am including these for the sake of completeness and in the hope that someone will try them.

Lesson 12: Bounces

In this lesson, I will be covering the three major kinds of Bounces: "Body Bounces," "Floor Bounces," and "Wall Bounces."

Body Bounces. Get yourself three balls that bounce well but are soft enough that you won't mind them hitting your body. A good choice would be sponge balls. In the Regular Cascade, the Exchange consists of a throw and then a catch. The Body Bounce is equivalent to a throw and a catch combined. The main difference is that the Exchange involves two different balls while the Bounce involves only one. The Body Bounce can be substituted for the Exchange anywhere it occurs, pro-

vided that the displaced ball is held in your hand or accommodated somehow.

Hand Bounce. Start a Regular Cascade, but then hold a ball in your right hand as the next throw comes to that hand. Bounce that incoming ball off the ball in your right hand, sending it back to your left hand. In the "Hand Bounce" you temporarily do not throw the ball in your right hand, instead you use it like a bat. You can also use the back of your hand, your wrist, your forearm, your elbow, or even your upper arm as a bat to hit a ball back to the other side. You can even hit it straight up in a Same-Hand Bounce.

Head Bounce. Use soft balls for this. To bounce anything off your head, the rule is: Keep your eyes on the ball as long as possible. This will insure that your head is in the right position. Don't throw the ball too high—just a little above your head is sufficient. Since you are throwing the ball to the centerline of your body, not to the other side, this throw must be much shorter and more vertical than a regular throw. After you have gained control of the Head Bounce, you can either bounce the ball back to the hand that threw it or to the other hand, and resume the Regular Cascade.

Knee and Foot Bounces. If your legs are really strong, and you have had no trouble with the Leg Throws, you should work on "Knee Bounces." Actually, this is really an "Upper-Leg" Bounce. Get your knee up high enough that your upper leg is level and the ball bounces away from you straight up, rather than forward. You should experiment to find the exact place on your leg to hit the ball so it goes where you want it to. If you are throwing with your right hand, you can bounce the ball off either the near leg or the far one, making it go on to your left hand or back to your right. Much more difficult, especially when you are using a small ball, is kicking the ball back up with your foot, so that you can continue juggling.

Body Bounce Practice. As you have seen in previous lessons, the Full-Shower is the goal toward which you can work. In most

Body-Bounce variations it is not possible to go all the way to a Full-Shower, since a bounce involves one ball, not two, and that other ball has to be taken care of. For instance, a Full-Shower of Knee Bounces can involve only one ball; to do it you would have to hold the other two balls in your hands.

Floor Bounces. Get yourself a set of hard balls that really bounce, such as lacrosse or dog balls. Experiment with these, bouncing them on a hard floor. You will notice that you will always have to add a little energy to them to make them come back up to the level from which you threw them. A ball that is simply dropped never comes all the way up to its original height; it always loses a little energy. By using live balls on a very hard floor, this loss of energy can be lessened, but is always present to some degree.

Lift and Push. There are two basic ways of adding the extra amount of energy you need—the "Lift" and the "Push." The Lift consists of throwing the ball up a short distance, then letting it fall and bounce. The Push is actually throwing the ball down forcibly at the floor. These two different kinds of throws result in two completely different kinds of paths through the air, and each produces its own Floor-Bounce variation. These are the "Lift Cascade" and the "Push Cascade." Imagine two spots on the floor in front of you, about shoulder-distance apart for the Lift Cascade, and about six inches apart for the Push Cascade. You can mark them with white tape.

Lift Cascade. The Lift produces an arc that climbs from your hand upward into the air and then descends to the floor and bounces back up into your hand. This path is several times longer than that of the Push, and so the time it takes is correspondingly longer. Because of the longer time, the sideways displacement of the ball is also greater, which tends to make the pattern become very wide. To keep this pattern from getting too wide, keep your hands close together and throw the balls almost straight up, as in the Narrow Pattern of juggling. Another way to reduce

the sideways motion is to bend down or kneel so that you are juggling close to the floor.

Start juggling, then let a ball thrown by your right hand continue to the floor by purposely not catching it with your left. This ball should land in the area of the left-hand mark on the floor. After it bounces up again, let it come down into your left hand and resume juggling. Remember that each ball from your right hand hits the left spot, and each ball from your left hand hits the right spot, so that the balls cross over each other as they fall. As you have done in several areas now, work toward eliminating the regular throws, and do more and more special throws until you are doing a Full Shower of Lift Cascading.

Push Cascade. The Push takes a much shorter path, between your hand and the floor and back up. Because it is shorter, a lot less time is required, and the rhythm is faster. The throws are much more forceful. It feels something like the Claw does, with your hand palm-down as you throw and catch. The energy of the Push calls for careful control. Here the ball hits the nearer of the two spots and bounces nearly straight up. Build toward doing all Push throws. One special problem in the Push Cascade is that there are certain moments when your hands block the view of the balls. You have to believe that the balls will still be there, even if you lose sight of them momentarily.

After you have perfected the Lift and Push Cascades, you should be able to switch from one to the other and even do mixed throws, as with the Overthrows and the Underthrows. Almost any variation you have already learned can be adapted to Floor Bounces. You might try bouncing balls off a large drum, which will help your rhythm and has some performing possibilities.

Wall Bounces. A necessary step in learning to pass balls with a partner is bouncing a ball off a wall in front of you. The wall temporarily takes the place of your partner. There are two basic types of Wall Bounces: "Same-Hand Bounces" and "Opposite-Hand Bounces," the easier of the two.

Stand about five or six feet from a good,

solid wall. Put two regular balls in your right hand and a red one in your left. The ball in your left hand is called a "Lead Ball" (rhymes with "bead"). It is called this because after it has been thrown to your right hand, it is always the first ball to be thrown at the wall or to your partner. This is a convention among jugglers, and I use it in this book. If you count every throw of your right hand, you will see that the Lead Ball is the third right-hand throw. The Lead Ball always means the single ball in your left hand, which will always be thrown from your right hand after it gets there.

Opposite-Hand Bounce. Start doing a Regular Cascade, and when the Lead Ball comes around, throw it underhanded up at the wall above the level of your head. In the beginning don't even worry about it bouncing back to you. Just get rid of it and try to catch the following ball coming in from your left hand. Of course, if you throw this ball away, you will have only two balls left and will have to stop juggling. If the bounced ball had come back into your left hand, you could have continued your volley. As you work more on wall bounces, you will see that the ball you throw up at the wall with your right hand will return and land in your left hand just in time for you to continue juggling without interrupting the rhythm.

The Lead Ball should hit the wall exactly at the top of its arc. It should be moving level as it hits the wall and bounces away again. After it hits, it should not continue upward or drop like a stone. In order to get that bounced ball to land in your left hand, you must hit the wall at a point opposite the centerline of your body. You will not be throwing straight ahead, but a little toward your left hand. In the Same-Hand Wall Bounce and in Ball Passing, the throw must be exactly straight ahead. Keep in mind the slight difference between these two throws, so that you don't get locked in on one way of throwing.

Now reverse the words left and right, so that you start with two balls in your left hand and the red ball in your right. Work on this side until it is as easy as the other. Eventually you will be able to throw every ball from both hands up against the wall (the Full-Shower again), so that no throws at all come directly across your body from hand to hand.

Same-Hand Bounce. One variation of the Wall Bounce involves throwing the ball absolutely straight ahead of your right hand up to the wall, from where it will eventually come back to your right hand. During this interim period, another ball will be coming to your right hand from your left and will be thrown back to it. Then the ball that was thrown at the wall returns to your right hand, and you go back into the Regular Cascade again. You can even combine Same-Hand and Opposite-Hand Throws. This Same-Hand Bounce is necessary to help you throw the ball straight out in front of your hand. Be sure to practice it with both your right and left hands.

Combinations. This concludes the work on the major patterns and variations based on the Regular Cascade for solo juggling (Lessons 7 through 12). You should try to combine all the material you have covered so far in any creative way you can. For instance, Clawing while Reverse Cascading is entirely possible. If you can whistle and dance while you do this, all the better. Bouncing the balls under your legs is another possible combination. You can combine any of this work with various body positions. Let your imagination run a little, and see what you can come up with. It is these and other personal variations that will help you to define your own style and way of juggling.

Tricks. There is an indistinct line dividing the good, solid variations, which aid physical training, body awareness, and concentration, and the various unending personal bits and "tricks" of the performing juggler. I have avoided as much as possible talking about these tricks. For one thing, there is simply an endless number of them and for another, these tricks amount to almost personal mannerisms, and therefore belong to each individual juggling style. Also, it is almost impossible to describe many of them. Finally, I emphasize that a good, solid training in the basic principles of juggling will lead you to work on your own mannerisms, as your own personality and preferences dictate.

Lesson 13: Beginnings & Endings

So far, you have used the Basket to accommodate the extra ball when beginning or ending a volley. There are, however, some other more interesting ways of handling the extra ball. This is the appropriate moment to present them, since they will be very useful as you progress to Ball Passing in the next lesson. The following ways to start and finish your volley give your work a more defined and polished look.

BEGINNINGS

Two-in-One-Hand. This is the easiest of the "Beginnings." Throw both balls in your right hand at the same time. Send them up a little higher than your normal juggling height and in such a way that they separate from each other. As they come down, throw the single ball in your left hand up in between or near the first two, and catch one of the falling balls in each hand at the same time. When the third ball comes down later, go in under it with your right hand holding its ball, and begin a Regular Cascade.

Three-in-One-Hand. After you have mastered the "Two-in-One-Hand" and have proficiency in Clawing, you will be ready to take on the "Three-in-One-Hand." Place all three balls in a triangle in your right hand, so that one ball is out on your fingertips. With your palm down, throw all three balls up in the air all at the same time. To do this, rotate your hand upward around an imaginary axis in your wrist, making the ball on your fingertips (the one furthest away from that axis) go higher than the other two. These will separate from each other, as in the Two-in-One-Hand. Practice just this much until you can throw the balls into a triangular pattern in the air. The fingertip ball will be the highest and in the middle; the other two balls will be lower, one on each side.

As soon as the two side balls reach the tops of their paths, Claw them quickly downward. Practice Clawing with your right and left hands individually for a while before you attempt to Claw with both at the same time. The idea here is to pull these two balls downward faster than they would normally fall. The third ball is still falling naturally. After you get the two balls down, turn your hands palms upward and bring your right hand in under the third ball, going into the Regular Cascade. If you can do this well, it has a spectacular effect. Make sure those you perform for see that all three balls are in your right hand before you start, or they will miss the point.

BOUNCE BEGINNINGS

Two-Ball-Bounce. A nice variation is to bounce the balls as you begin. You should find a level floor surface for this. Hold two balls in your right hand so that there is about a half-inch space between them. Hold your hand palm-down with the two balls absolutely level with each other (at the same height above the floor). Now, as you throw these balls down to the floor, bring your hand straight down, keeping it perfectly level, like an elevator in a shaft. You must come down absolutely straight. If you do it right, the balls will be about a foot apart when they come up again from the floor. They should be thrown hard enough so that they come up to the Tray Plane or higher. As they hover at the top of their paths, bring the third ball in your left hand in under the ball on the left and go into the Regular Cascade. Throw the balls carefully; this is a very easy one to miss. If one ball gets too close to the other on the way to the floor, they will collide and go shooting off like a couple of scared mice.

Three-Ball Bounce. Now you are getting into the graduate work of Beginnings. Put all three balls in your right hand, with a half-inch space between them all around. Hold your hand palm down with all three balls absolutely level. Come down toward the floor with enough force to get the balls back up where you can reach them. Then, as you did in the non-bounce Three-in-One-Hand, Claw two balls down from the tops of their paths, letting the third one drop by itself. You will find this easier if you practice the non-bounce version without adding any extra height to the

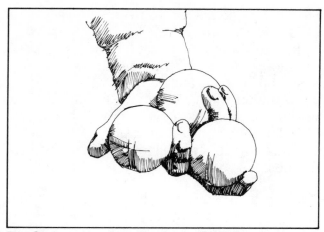

The Grab, or hand position for holding three balls

center ball. After a while you will be able to give the fingertip ball an extra push as you throw the balls down, thus making it go higher than the other two. As the balls come back to your Tray Plane, pick the lower two to Claw. You can also Claw these two before they reach their highest point. The third ball will continue on up. When it comes down again, go into the Regular Cascade.

Three-Misses Bounce. Start with the balls in the normal way, two in your right hand and one in your left. But as you start juggling, throw each ball much higher and more nearly straight up than usual (Narrow Pattern). Let each ball bounce on the floor once ("missing" them). Then catch them in the same order you threw them, (and they bounced), and go into the Regular Cascade. Use balls of three different colors so that you can calculate which you should be catching first, second, and third. If you go after them in the same order you threw them, you will find that each will be coming up just as you need it. The first will be on your left, the second on your right, and the third on your left again.

If you were to do a normal-width Cascade to start, the balls would be about six feet apart by the time they had gone up, come down to the floor, gone back up, and come down into your hands again. Therefore, remember that now you have to start with your hands closer together and throw the balls more straight up, using the Narrow Pattern that you already know. Also, a higher throw is necessary to give the balls enough energy to bounce back up to your hands. This variation can be inserted in the middle of your juggling, as well as at the beginning. It can also be used to cover up a mistake if you think fast enough. However, most people don't mind seeing you make a mistake.

Miscellaneous Beginnings. Where you get the balls from can determine a whole range of other beginnings. Someone in the audience, or an assistant, can throw three balls to you. Make sure they throw them almost straight up, so you can catch them. You can pick the balls off a table one at a time, or you can take a ball out from under your chin, one out of your pocket, and one from your hat. You can even throw a ball up from your back by first letting it roll down over your head and then suddenly snapping your neck up. There is virtually no end of possible variations, and you will enjoy investigating them.

ENDINGS

"Endings" are like the punctuation at the end of a sentence; they finish the action in a definite way. A good flashy Ending will trigger a lot of applause from those watching, if that's what interests you. There is a club equivalent of each of the ball endings, in addition to many other possible ball variations.

High-Throw Ending. When you want to end a volley, do one slow High Throw from your right hand. It should go about four or five feet above your head, depending on how high the ceiling is. If you are outdoors, you will have a little more room. While it is up in the air, transfer the ball in your right hand to your left by bringing your two hands together. This will leave your right hand empty to catch the final ball. The most important catch is the last one, and having your hand empty helps you to make sure that you don't miss this last ball. To cover yourself if you do miss, just let the ball bounce once before catching it. Make sure that those watching know that you intended to do this, so it won't look like a miss.

Spin Ending. One variation of the High-Throw ending is to spin yourself around once after you catch the last ball. If you grab it with an Inward-Sideways Claw, your right hand across to your left, the momentum of your arm will carry you around one full turn counterclockwise. This will easily carry you into a show-bizzy bow to the assembled cheering multitudes. The effect of the sudden disappearance of all the balls, and of you for a moment, is quite impressive.

Run Ending. Using the High-Throw Ending, throw the last ball out ahead of you rather than straight up. As you do this, switch the next ball to your left hand, and then run after the last ball and catch it.

With a few exceptions, an ending should always follow a short volley of Regular Cascade, indicating that you did something special that has now been concluded. Each variation is like a "figure" displayed against the "ground" of the Regular Cascade.

From now on in your work, you should always use one of these endings so that they become built in. When working with partners, as we will see in the next lesson, the ending will be an indication to both of you that you were together and stayed together during the entire volley.

Lesson 14: Ball-Passing

Some jugglers believe that passing objects between two partners is the real heart of juggling, and I agree. But when you do ball passing, you will find that your throw is going to have to be somewhat different. Now you will be throwing straight out ahead of you. In order not to destroy your Cascade juggling, where you worked very hard to throw the ball sideways to your left hand, you should not work on this lesson until your Cascade is in perfect shape.

If you haven't done so already, you should now get a real, live partner. He or she should be someone who has been over this same material and has reached a comparable degree of skill. If your partner is way ahead or way behind you, it will be much more difficult to work with him. As soon as you start juggling with a partner, you will be exposed to a whole new area of consciousness. Although he becomes a part of your mechanical system, he is also separated from you. He has a style and rhythm of his own, which, at least in the beginning, is totally unknown to you. You and your partner will have to be very conscientious and careful about what is going on; each of you will have to have the utmost patience and consideration for the other.

You should have six balls, all the same weight and size. Two of them might be a different color, say red.

Tuning-In. You and your partner should practice together a lot, so that each of you can adjust to the rhythms and throwing habits of the other. I suggest that in the beginning you always try to work with the same partner. Later, you will be able to adjust much more quickly to someone new. Half-Juggling, which you have already seen, is an excellent practice for tuning-in.

Symmetry Exercise. The following exercise is a really fine way of learning to adjust to your partner. Stand facing your partner, about three feet in front of him, each of you juggling your own three balls. Try to keep your hands level with his, and throw the balls to the same height. If you do this for a while, you will find out that both of you will be able to lock into the same rhythm. If you look closely at your own pattern and then at your partner's, you will see that this coordination of rhythm can take place in two different ways: (1) Your right hand and your partner's left hand, directly opposite, are throwing balls at the same instant. This gives the feeling of being in front of a mirror and is called "Mirror Symmetry." (2). Your right hand and your partner's right hand are throwing at the same time. This is like shaking hands. If you were to turn around with your back to your partner while juggling, the pattern and rhythm of each of you would be absolutely identical. This is called "Turn-Around Symmetry."

Phase. Mirror Symmetry, where your right hand is throwing simultaneously with your partner's left, can be called "Out-of-Phase Tuning." Turn-Around Symmetry, right hand with right hand, is called "In-Phase Tuning." Later, when you start passing, you will see the reason for these designations.

Tuning Practice. Face your partner and both start juggling. You will find by experimenting with your rhythms that you can slow down and speed up relative to your partner's juggling. This means that you can go from In-Phase to Out-of-Phase Tuning and back at will. If you want to speed up your rhythm to catch up with your partner, throw the balls lower. To slow down your rhythm, so that he can catch up to you, throw the balls higher. It is a good practice to designate one of you as the "Leader" to keep a steady rhythm, and let the other, the "Follower," do the speeding up or slowing down. Then you can reverse roles. Do this practice until you feel in harmony with your partner.

Downbeat. Sooner or later the problem of starting together will arise, just as it does with musicians who have to work together in the same rhythm. Jugglers make an agreement that they will always start in a certain way. In this book I use a convention that is followed by many jugglers: face each other, and bring your hands (with the balls or other objects you are going to juggle) up to your shoulders. Then immediately come down to Home Position and start to juggle. These raising and lowering motions create two beats that define the beginning of the volley and set the speed and rhythm. It is also a nice kind of salute or greeting to your partner, and it is an indication that you are both ready to begin. The Follower may bring his hands up to shoulder height and hold them there, waiting for the Leader to bring his hands up to the same place and down again to start the volley. In the case of three- or four-partner formations, it must be done this way, since there will be several Followers waiting for the Leader to give the signal to begin. There is a neatness and polish to this Downbeat gesture, and it creates an energy that helps you and your partner quickly tune in to the rhythm of the particular pattern or variation you are doing.

Throughout this lesson and in the lesson on Club Passing, I will be referring to "you" and "your partner." You should switch roles constantly in each of the lessons. Taking both roles for each point will help both of you to understand what your partner is going through at any given moment.

Jump-In. In this first exercise, have your partner take the role of Leader and begin a Regular Cascade, while you wait without juggling. Watch his right-hand throws and try to get the feel of the rhythm. Then, as he makes a throw with his right hand, make your first throw to yourself with your right hand, and go directly into a Regular Cascade. If you haven't lost the beat, you will find that the two of you are maintaining In-Phase rhythm. Once you get into In-Phase and feel the pace of it, it is very easy to stay there indefinitely.

False-Start. One helpful way of getting your first throw in at the right time, without losing the beat, is to watch your partner's right hand and make a series of "False-Start Throws." Do this in time to his throws, but do not let go of the ball. When you feel ready, let a ball go exactly on the beat, and you will be in In-Phase rhythm from the beginning without having to do much adjusting. By doing this exercise, you will establish a good rapport and awareness with your partner.

Throw-In. Stand facing your partner, about four feet in front of him. Place one ball in each hand. Your partner should have a red ball in his right hand. He throws this ball straight across to your left hand, throwing it up to the same height as his own regular juggling. Just before this ball comes down to your left hand, throw the ball that is there to your right hand and start a Regular Cascade. This is the basic "Throw-In," a fairly simple exercise. You have seen it before in the work on Bounces.

Throw-Out. This time, stand in front of your partner and have a red ball in your left hand and the other two balls in your right. This solitary ball in your left hand is called the Lead Ball, as you may remember from the lesson on Wall Bounces. Your partner is empty-handed. Start juggling, and pass the Lead Ball to your partner after it comes around to your right hand. As in Wall Bounces, the Lead Ball will be the fifth ball if you count right-hand throws only. From now on, we will be counting only right-hand throws. "Throwing to your partner" will now be referred to as "Passing."

Throw the passed ball straight ahead of you in an arc exactly the same height as the throws to your own left hand. It should land in your partner's left hand, as it does when he is in Home Position. Do not throw it to the level of his shoulder. He should not have to claw the ball to catch it, and if he does, it is your error, not his. All throws should "peak" or reach their highest point at eye-level, exactly midway between you and your partner. After you have thrown this ball, you will have only two left, and so you will have to stop juggling. Work on this "Throw Out" until you can throw the Lead Ball absolutely straight ahead of your right hand and make it land in your partner's hand. Your other throws should still be straight across you, close to your body. And don't miss the next ball coming from your own left hand. This catch ends the volley.

Throw-In-and-Out. In this next stage, you will be combining the Throw-In and the Throw-Out. Start exactly as you did for the Throw-In, with one ball in each hand and your partner with a red ball in his right hand. Your partner throws his red ball to you (Throw-In); you catch it and begin to juggle. When the red ball gets to your right hand, pass it back to him (Throw-Out). He transfers the red ball back to his right hand by throwing it across in rhythm, and he is ready to throw in to you again. You can see that the red ball makes a little circuit as it passes between you and your partner. Make sure that you take both roles.

A good exercise to do using the Throw-In-and-Out is to take three balls and give two to your partner. The ball in your left hand should be red. Pass this red Lead Ball across to your partner. He catches it and starts juggling; you have stopped. You have done a Throw-Out, while he received a Throw-In. When the red ball gets around to his right hand, he will be doing a Throw-Out as far as he is concerned, but it will be a Throw-In to you. This red ball can continue to go around

the circle between you and your partner indefinitely.

Half-Passing. This exercise uses four balls, two of them red. In the Throw-In-and-Out exercise, if your partner had kept a second red ball in his right hand all along, he could have passed another ball to you much sooner. In fact, with a second ball, he can throw one to you at exactly the same moment you are throwing one to him. You would be *getting* a Throw-In at the same time you were *doing* a Throw-Out, and you wouldn't have to stop juggling or make any break in the rhythm. In order for this to be rhythmical, your partner should be throwing a red ball over to his right hand at the same time you throw your red ball to your right hand before passing it. This is called "Half-Passing," because you are juggling while your partner is only catching and throwing the red balls. At this point, you are only one step away from actually passing balls.

Work on these exercises with your partner long enough that each of you can go on indefinitely in either role. Start with the Throw-In-and-Out, then do the Five-Ball Passing, and work up to Half-Passing, which could be called a Simultaneous Throw-In-and-Out. The partner not juggling should throw the red ball—not hand it—across from his left hand to his right, in rhythm with the other red ball.

Full-Passing. If you succeeded in doing the Half-Passing, Full-Passing should be fairly easy. The only difference is that your partner is also juggling while he is throwing to you and receiving from you. Since, in Half-Passing, you have been throwing and catching from your partner while juggling, it shouldn't be too difficult to have your partner do this too. Try it. Use the Downbeat to get started together. In the beginning you will both probably blow up a lot. Stick to it. You will observe that you and your partner are both doing exactly the same thing now, passing balls.

Every Third. In the beginning you should do a single pass (one ball thrown each way simultaneously), recover your juggling, and then stop the volley. Later, each of you starts with a red ball (the Lead Ball) in your left hand. Each time this ball comes around to your right hand, pass it to your partner, and he will be passing one to you at the same time. You will find that the rhythm, counting right-hand throws only, goes: PASS, Self, Self; PASS, Self, Self; PASS, Self, Self; and so on. This pattern is called passing Every Third. In all formations the first ball passed is always the Lead Ball. Before the first pass there are two preliminary Selfs from your right hand, which are not usually counted in the Passing pattern. Therefore, the Lead Ball really defines the beginning of any particular pattern. It is very important from now on that you and your partner keep your eyes on each other, especially when either of you bends down to pick up a dropped ball. Never throw any object to your partner unless he knows you are throwing it and is ready to catch it.

Every Other. Work for a while on Every Third, passing the red ball each time. Always plan each thing you are going to do with your partner before you start. This is an important part of learning to work together. After you are satisfied with Every Third, get six balls of the same color, or three pairs of balls—two reds, two greens, and two blues—or just ignore the colors altogether. This time you will be passing every other ball that comes to your right hand. The rhythm is more dense, since there are more passes in a given number of throws. It goes: One ball to your partner, one ball to yourself, and so on. The beginning of every Passing Pattern is always the same, and the Lead Ball is always the first pass. The rhythm, counting right-hand throws only, is PASS, Self; PASS, Self; PASS, Self; and so on.

If you and your partner use a set of red, green, and blue balls, as suggested, start with them in the same places in your hands. Now, the colors of each pair of passed balls will be the same. If you see two balls of different colors going across, it means there is something wrong.

Showering. An even more advanced step is the "Shower," which is really a Half-Shower in the terms I have been using. Here, your right hand never throws anything back to your left hand (a "Self"). Every ball from your right hand is passed to your partner. They all come from your partner, land in your left hand, are thrown across to your right, and then are passed from your right hand back to your partner. The balls run around on a kind of circular track between you and your partner. The Passing Pattern here is a simple PASS; PASS; PASS; PASS; and so on.

Twosies. If you are having trouble doing longer series of Showers, try this exercise. It is a compromise between Showering and Every Other. "Twosies" is the name my teacher gave it. The Passing Pattern consists of alternating Showers with Every Others, and it looks like this: PASS; PASS, Self; PASS; PASS, Self; PASS; PASS, Self; and so on. It's a kind of waltz-time rhythm.

Many other rhythms can be worked out. You might find completely irregular rhythms, patterns in which the passes increase in number, or patterns taken from the beat of songs. Always remember to go over what you are going to do with your partner and agree before you begin. This will allow you to work more harmoniously together and save you a lot of energy in misunderstandings.

Ending. You have learned how to end a volley of solo juggling with a High-Throw Ending. Now you will learn how to end a volley of ball passing. A good, clean simultaneous ending by two partners is a thing of beauty to behold. Practice doing just one pass, then throw two more Selfs with your right hand. Then on the next right-hand throw, do the High-Throw Ending. Endings should be cushioned from the variations that preceded them by throwing exactly two Selfs, no more and no less, and then the High-Throw Ending. This gives your audience time to see what you are doing.

Passing Unit. This is any group of throws consisting of one pass to your partner followed by any number of throws to yourself, from zero Selfs on up to four or five. Each Pass starts a new "Passing Unit." For instance, the first two Passing Units in the Every-Third pattern would be PASS, Self, Self; PASS, Self, Self. This is two Passing Units of three throws each. If some other pattern should follow, you must still throw the two final Selfs of the Every Third before starting the Passing Unit of the next pattern.

The only exception to this is the Ending throw, which is always preceded by just two Selfs, regardless of what came before. Also, at the beginning, just before the Lead Ball there is an incomplete Passing Unit of just two Selfs.

Three-Three-Ten. You are now ready to combine all the material that has been covered in this lesson into one composite "Passing Sequence." This one is called the "Three-Three-Ten." It consists of three passes Every Third, three passes Every Other, ten Showers, and an Ending. In the following diagram each Passing Unit is on a separate line. The Beginning and Ending are special units, as indicated earlier. The accompanying chart shows the way the Passing Sequence looks.

THREE-THREE-TEN PASSING SEQUENCE

Self, Self;	Incomplete Passing Unit before Lead Ball
Pass, Self, Self;	Three Passes Every Third
Pass, Self, Self;	
Pass, Self, Self;	
Pass, Self;	Three Passes Every Other
Pass, Self;	
Pass, Self;	
Pass;	Ten Showers
Pass;	
Pass;	
Pass;	
Pass;	
Pass;	
Pass;	
Pass;	
Pass;	
Pass;	
Self, Self, HIGH.	High-Throw Ending

Three-Three-Ten Practice. In order for you to build up properly to this Passing Sequence, and so that you don't bite off more than you can chew, I suggest you first work through the following progression of simpler sequences. Each of these will give you an intermediate goal against which you can measure your progress. You and your partner should agree in advance on which of these steps you will be working on at any time. "Ending" here refers to the whole Passing Unit of Self, Self, High Throw Ending.

1. One Pass plus an Ending
2. Three Every Third plus an Ending
3. Three Every Other plus an Ending
4. Three Showers plus an Ending
5. Five Showers plus an Ending
6. Seven Showers plus an Ending
7. Ten Showers plus an Ending
8. Three Every Third plus three Every Other plus an Ending
9. Three Every Third plus three Every Other plus three Showers plus an Ending
10. Three Every Third plus three Every Other plus five Showers plus and Ending
11. Three Every Third plus three Every Other plus seven Showers plus an Ending
12. Three Every Third plus three Every Other plus ten Showers plus an Ending

Idling and Signaling. An advanced way to begin juggling is for both you and your partner to juggle In-Phase but without doing any passing. Juggling without passing or doing any special throws is called "Idling." On any given throw from his right hand, the Leader calls "Hup" as a signal to do something special. Then you each let the next two throws from your right hands (Selfs) go back to yourselves, continuing to juggle. On the next right-hand throw, begin some agreed-upon Passing Pattern. It may be passing; it may be an Ending, or you may just shout and run out of the room. The Passing Pattern is counted: Hup, Self, Self, GO. Idling and Signaling allow you to start juggling, talk over what you might do, and then do it. If you don't do an Ending, you can decide on something else without stopping the volley. The count for an Ending would be: HUP, Self, Self, HIGH. Always allow two intervening Selfs to give your partner time to react. When performing, the "hups" should be very quiet. If you wish, you can devise some other signal. Try starting off with a Jump-In, described earlier. Your partner is juggling. You come along, see him, get out three balls, and start juggling in front of him. On the signal, do your thing. This is really good stuff for performing.

The fastest way to learn the Three-Three-Ten sequence is to agree with your partner to work together and not stop until you have done each of the sequences that you planned to do. Then plan to keep on going until you have done one successful Three-Three-Ten volley. Even if you have become exhausted, continue to work. It is often in this exhausted state that old habits and blocks wear out and are discarded. When you have done one successful Three-Three-Ten after a long hard period of work, quit right away. Success results from setting a goal and not stopping until it is reached. But once it is reached, you should stop immediately, forget about juggling, and do something else. The connections have been made; your task is done for the moment.

The next practice session will probably show that you have slipped back. But after warming up you will be able to get back again, and much faster this time. When warming up, always go through some of the twelve steps listed in the chart. Even after you have had years of juggling experience, it will still take fifteen or twenty minutes to warm up and tune yourself in to what you are doing.

The Three-Three-Ten Passing Sequence is a kind of gauge of how good your ball passing is at any moment. It covers a variety of skills. After you and your partner have done it well many times, you should try working on it with other partners. Eventually you will be able to pass balls with almost any experienced juggler who comes along. After only a few minutes' time to acquaint yourselves with each other's styles, you both will be juggling well together. When you feel sufficiently skilled in ball passing, go on to the next lesson.

Lesson 15: Ball-Passing Variations

Once you and your partner have established a solid rhythmic ball-passing pattern, there is almost no end to the variations that you can develop. I will cover a number of them in this lesson.

Cage. Have a third person stand between you and your partner while you are passing balls. Your passes go on one side of this person, and your partner's passes come back on the other. Have the person in the middle stand sideways, so you will have room and be able to see better. For safety, he should be turned so that the throws of the more-experienced juggler pass by his face. This third person might be juggling, too, or doing something besides just standing there. You should stand a little further apart than for regular ball passing.

Shooting Gallery. A third person can also run back and forth across the path of the balls between you and your partner. With a little practice, he can run through even when the two of you are rapidly showering every ball. He runs a split-second after the balls have gone by the center of the space between you. The two jugglers should stand a little further apart to make room. The runner should face his left, so that he won't be hit in the face if he doesn't get all the way through.

Box. For this variation you need four jugglers. Stand in a square and pass balls with the person opposite, while the people on your left and right are passing with each other. All four start juggling together, but the second pair of jugglers will start passing one right-hand throw later than the usual Lead-Ball pass. Everyone should be using the Every-Other Passing Pattern, so that while one team is passing, the other team is throwing a Self, and vice versa. A fifth brave person can stand in this box, as with the "Cage." He should stand diagonally, to present the least silhouette, and he should stand very still and close his eyes.

Feed. Here you need at least three jugglers, and it is possible to do it with five or six. Let us assume there are three. One person is designated the Leader. He stands facing the other two, who are standing side by side. The juggler to the Leader's left is called Number One, and the other juggler is Number Two. All three start juggling together. The first pass is between only the Leader and Number One. The Leader's second pass is to Number Two while Number One throws a Self. Then the Leader passes to Number One again, and he continues to alternate between the two. The Leader is Showering, while each of the other jugglers is doing Every Other passing in counter-rhythm to each other.

In the beginning, the Leader counts off, "One, two, one, two," and so on, just as his passes are thrown. The other two jugglers pass as their numbers are called. With three people and a Leader, the counting goes, "One, two, three, two, one, two, three," and so on, moving back and forth along the line. When you have three or more jugglers in the line, it is especially important to have everyone at the same distance from the Leader, forming an arc around him. Each juggler should stand far enough away from his neighbors that there is no collision of hands and arms as they juggle.

Triangle. In a "Triangle," there are three jugglers, and no Leader. Each of the three jugglers passes at the same time, just as if there were only two people doing regular passing. The main difficulty is the wide angle between the ball that you are passing and the ball that you are receiving. As soon as you pass to your partner, you will have to look around quickly for the incoming ball. Any Passing pattern or sequence can be used for this, including the Three-Three-Ten.

Drop-Back. The "Drop-Back" uses only three balls. This is more of a Give-Away than a passing formation, and it serves as a preparation for the "Line-Passing Formation" to be discussed. Your partner stands about three feet behind you. You start to juggle, and as soon as the Lead Ball reaches your right hand, you throw it over your left shoulder. You will have to experiment with just how to do this so your partner can catch it. Generally, you don't have to give it much more impetus than a regular pass. Don't let it go too wide.

There are two ways the remaining balls can be dropped back. One is for you to throw all three balls from your right hand as they arrive there. This is called "Slow-Succession Passing." A faster way to make the transfer is to throw the balls from your right, left, and right hands alternately in what is called "Quick-Succession Passing." For the "Line-Passing" variation, you will be making all the throws from your right hand over your left shoulder in Slow Succession.

Drop-Forward. The reverse of the Drop-Back is the "Drop-Forward." Here you send the balls forward to your partner who is standing a few feet in front of you with his back to you. The balls should be thrown vertically and quite high, coming down fairly wide to the side and well ahead of him. The Receiver should not look to the side, but he can tilt his head upward so he can see the balls early enough. With good timing and accurate placement of the balls, the Receiver will soon know where to expect them. Use either Quick or Slow Succession. In Slow Succession, remember not to throw the first ball caught until the second one almost arrives.

Line Passing. Here the Leader faces a line of jugglers, who are standing one behind the other as though waiting on line. They all start juggling together. The Leader passes to Number One on line, whom he is facing. Simultaneously, Number One drops a ball with his right hand back over his left shoulder to Number Two. Number Two drops a ball back to Number Three, and so on. The last juggler on the line passes a ball all the way forward to the Leader. All these passes happen simultaneously. You can use any Passing Pattern or Sequence, including the Three-Three-Ten.

Run-Around. Two people are passing balls. A "Robber" comes along and stands to the left of one of the jugglers (the "Victim"). The Robber starts intercepting and catching with his left hand the passes that should be coming to the victim's left hand. The juggler opposite aids the Robber by throwing the balls wider so that he can get them. After three such catches, the Victim has nothing left to juggle with, and the Robber is passing the balls. The Victim now runs across and stands to the left of his former partner, intercepting the balls as they come near him. Victim has turned Robber, and the process continues, with each person running around to the other end. The Passing Pattern used is Showering, and it is necessary to *run* to get to the other end before the next ball arrives there. This formation is especially effective with clubs because club jugglers stand further apart than ball jugglers. Half-Juggling is also possible at one or both ends of the formation; three or four people can be involved, each Half-Juggler using only one hand.

Partial Passing. This term refers to two jugglers passing with fewer than six balls. Half-Juggling, the Drop-Back, and the Drop-Forward, as well as the Take-Away and the Give-Away to be covered in the next lesson, are all examples of Partial Passing in which only three balls are used. The Slow and Quick Succession Transfers also use three balls.

Slow-Succession Transfer. Juggle three balls while your partner stands empty-handed. Then Shower all three balls one at a time from your right hand to your partner, so that *you* are now empty-handed. Your partner passes the first ball he received back to you on the next beat, as if you were both Showering. Remember to throw the Set-Up ball from your left hand first, before the second pass with your right hand. While it is easy to get your three throws off in an even rhythm, it is harder to carry that same rhythm across from you to your partner and back in a smooth and regular way. The rhythm should be exactly even: THROW • THROW • THROW • throw • throw • throw (the uppercase words represent one partner, the lowercase words the other). This "Slow-Succession Transfer" is similar to the Throw-In and the Throw-Out.

Quick-Succession Transfer. Here, instead of throwing right-right-right, you will be throwing right-*left*-right, which gets the balls transferred much faster. You pass the first ball normally from your right hand. The second pass will be from your left hand to your partner's right hand, and the third pass will be from your right hand again. All three passes go straight across into the mirror-image hands of your partner. In the beginning, you can do a little idling between each transfer. After a while, you and your partner can reduce the amount of idling between transfers, so that the balls are flying back and forth between you like machine-gun fire. This exericse will give you some practice in passing with your left hand and catching with your right, something that many jugglers tend to neglect but which is important from the standpoint of equal development of both sides of your body. Later, you can modify the Quick- or Slow-Succession Transfers so that the throws are

all corner throws, going across diagonally from right to right hands, or left to left, criss-crossing each other. You can even learn to do regular six-ball passing with corner throws.

Four-Ball Transfer. There are a number of ways to arrange this variation. The easiest is to consider that you are juggling and passing four balls out of a possible six. You take three balls, and your partner has one in his right hand. You start with the Throw-In-and-Out. Both of you Shower all the balls that come to you from that point on, just as you did in the Slow-Succession Transfer.

Five-Ball Transfer. This is similar to the Four-Ball Transfer, except that now there is just one empty slot in the six-ball Passing Pattern of normal Showering. You take three balls, your partner takes two. You pass your Lead Ball. The partner who has two balls at any moment will have to Vamp (see below) until he receives a third ball game.

Seven- and Eight-Ball Passing. These are advanced variations. Each partner (or *one* of you if there are seven balls), will be starting with four balls, two in each hand. In both variations, you pass the balls very high. The person or persons with four balls has to get the second pass off before the first one lands in his partner's hand.

For Seven-Ball Passing only *you* have the extra ball. There is no Lead Ball, there are no preliminary Selfs; unlike in other passing, you go right into the Showering Pattern with the first ball thrown. You throw your first pass, and then you throw another before your first one gets to your partner. He throws his first pass after your first but before your second, so that there is an alternating rhythm between your partner's throws and yours. You and your partner never throw at the same time. Make sure that you throw very high, making room on the path for the seventh ball.

In Eight-Ball Passing each juggler starts with four balls, and each of you has to get off two passes before the first one lands in your partner's hand. You are now juggling with simultaneous passes again, as in regular Six-Ball Passing. The energy here is, of course, very much higher than in regular passing.

Lesson 16: Take-Aways & Give-Aways

In this lesson you are going to "steal" balls from another person while he is juggling. You will be the Robber, and he will be the Victim. A nicer word for stealing is "Take-Away," which is the term I will be using. Your debt to society will be repaid after you learn the Give-Away, which is the reverse of the Take-Away.

TAKE-AWAYS

Face-To-Face. You happen by and notice that your Victim is juggling three balls, and you think that *you'd* like to be juggling them. If you were to try to overpower him physically, the balls would probably roll all over the place in the struggle, and you might not be able to find all of them. Instead of this, go up to him and stand in front of him face-to-face. (It may take some practice for him to keep juggling while you come up close with the intention of pulling some "fast stuff.")

First catch. Now watch his right hand. Pick one of his throws. As soon as the ball leaves his right hand and reaches the top of its arc, or peaks, scoop it upward with your right hand, using an Upward Claw. Pull your hand out of his juggling pattern immediately so that the next ball doesn't hit your hand, and hold on to the ball you have. Keep your hands well above his Tray Plane, which might be at a different height from yours, and also above the highest point that his hands might come to as he throws. If your hand is too low, you might claw his hand along with the ball.

Second Catch. A moment later the second ball, from his left hand, will arrive at the peak. Claw this upward with your left hand, and hold on to this one also. These first two Upward Claws seem to take place at almost the same moment.

Third Catch. After the third ball, from his right hand again, reaches its peak, bring your right hand with its ball in under it as it falls, and go into a Regular Cascade.

Avoid false-starts, or giving your Victim any cue or warning of what you are going to do. Your Victim, of course, must not change or stop his juggling as you steal from him. He must not try to help you in any way, such as by throwing the balls to you or not trying to catch them, so that you can get them. He should continue to juggle exactly as if you were not there at all. However, his pattern should be fairly high and wide, and he should keep his hands down in the Tray Plane, out of your way, so you don't scratch his knuckles.

In order to learn this fully, both of you should work in both roles, Robber becoming Victim, and vice versa, until the Take-Away goes completely smoothly. The order of the balls taken is always that of the Quick Succession, right-left-right.

Side-By-Side. This is a more difficult variation. Stand to the left side of your Victim, facing roughly in the same direction as he but a little toward your right, toward his pattern. Stand very close to him, with your feet close together. Your right foot should point toward him and be in front of his left foot, in preparation for stepping across in front of him.

Since you are now facing in the same direction he is, rather than facing him, his hands will be in the reverse position from the Face-to-Face variation. Ignore the juggler completely; just look at the pattern of the balls and you will be doing the same thing as in Face-to-Face. The only problem is reaching and getting your hands in there and back out again without blowing the juggling.

First be aware of the space between your Victim's pattern and his chest. If he is juggling properly, there will be about eight inches of space, roughly equivalent to the length of his forearms, and his forearms themselves will be level. To get ready to do the Take-Aways, bring both your hands up to your chest level, and be prepared to spring.

First Catch. Pick a throw from his right hand, then reach into that open space with your left hand. Reach into his pattern and grab that ball, somewhere above his left hand. Immediately pull your hand back into the open space to keep it from being hit by the next throw.

Second Catch. A split second later, go across your Victim's chest with your right hand, and reach into his pattern just above his right hand, grabbing the ball that is arriving there. Also pull this hand out of his pattern.

Third Catch. The third throw will be coming from your Victim's right hand. Wait for it to go past the peak and come down a little. Then bring your left hand with its ball in under it, and go into a Regular Cascade.

In order to do this smoothly, you should be gently nudging your Victim out of his spot with your back and right shoulder, as you step across in front of him. He should be ready to step back, but he should not react in any visible way to your intrusion. He should continue to juggle as if nothing were happening and until he has no balls left.

Of course, you should work on taking-away from your Victim's right side as well as from his left. Just reverse the words "left" and "right" in the above discussion. If you remember that it is always your outside hand that takes the first ball, the rest will soon fall into place.

Take-Away Practice. To progress to either the Face-to-Face or the Side-by-Side, start by doing just the first catch. Don't worry about the other two balls. Then take away two of the balls, letting the third one go. Eventually, you will be able to take all three. After you have perfected these variations, the two of you can repeatedly take from one another on either side or face-to-face, without ever stopping the juggling. As you continue to improve, work toward taking away sooner and sooner from each other, so that only a few throws come between one Take-Away and the next. Take-Aways can be done with almost any kind of juggling, such as Bounces or Reverse Cascades.

Half-Take-Aways. The "Half-Take-Away" is a hybrid of a Take-Away and Half-Juggling. You go in as if to do a Take-Away but using only your outside hand, so that you and your partner end up doing Face-to-Face or Side-by-Side Half-Juggling. Later you can complete the Take-Away in a kind of delayed-reaction maneuver. It makes it all the more interesting

if your partner does not know what you are planning to do, and vice versa. You both have to keep very loose in order not to blow the whole thing.

Vamping. If you take just one ball from your Victim and walk away, you will leave him with two. He can continue with these two as if nothing happened. This will mean that he is juggling with two real balls and one imaginary one. This is called "Vamping." To learn this, have your partner take just one ball from you, and try to keep on juggling with the other two.

You will find that if you make one of the two remaining balls a red ball, you will be able to see a certain definite pattern to this Vamping. One ball will be thrown from your right hand, and the other will immediately follow from your left. Then there will be a pause. Then there will be a ball thrown from your *left* hand, immediately followed by one from your right. Then another pause, and this alternation of sides repeats. The same ball is thrown from each side alternately. The pause between Vamps is the imaginary ball. Note the spot from which the ball was taken; it is the place where that same ball or any other object must be thrown back in to restore the juggling.

Substitutions. If your Victim is Vamping properly, you can throw in or "Substitute" any object you want fairly easily. It must be timed right, or your Victim will have no chance of getting it back into his pattern.

Opposite-Hand Substitution. Stand to the right of your Victim, and hold the ball you are going to throw in under his right hand, a little closer to his centerline, so that there is room to throw it. He is Vamping. After he throws the first ball of the Vamp with his right hand and the second ball immediately from his left, there will be a pause during which he is throwing the imaginary ball. You will actually see his hand unoccupied at this moment, and he can wiggle his fingers or snap them without interrupting his rhythm. Throw your ball in only during this pause. It will go into the empty "slot" and enter his pattern. You should throw it across to his left hand, just as if he had thrown it himself. Since the ball you are throwing is part of an Exchange, the incoming ball of that Exchange can tell you when to throw. The incoming ball is the second ball of his Vamp and is coming from his left hand.

Since this is a little complicated, I will recapitulate. Each group of two throws is called a Vamp. A right-handed Vamp is one whose first throw is from the right hand. Your Victim is Vamping, which means that he is throwing alternate right-handed and left-handed Vamps or pairs of throws. If you are on his right side, you will throw in after his right-handed Vamp. The second throw of his right-handed Vamp will land back in his right hand, and you are to throw your ball in just before this ball lands so that you can form an Exchange with it. The rhythm pattern will be THROW (his) • THROW-CATCH • Substitute (you)CATCH. If you still can't figure this out, do what I did: Just try it all different ways until you hit on it.

Same-Hand Substitution. In this variation you throw your ball to the same side of your Victim that you are standing on, rather than across to his other hand. Here, you have to keep your hand outside of his. Perhaps the easiest way to understand this is simply to imagine that you are on the opposite side and are throwing across, using the method given above. You will be throwing after an opposite-side Vamp.

Stand-Behind. This is a substitution in which the object thrown in is never caught by the Victim. Stand directly behind him. Then reach around to the right, above his hands, and steal one ball. He Vamps the remaining two balls. You throw the ball back into his pattern as though it were a Substitution from the right. Then you quickly reach around to his left side and catch that same ball and throw it back as he would have done. Continue this way. Your Victim never gets to touch the ball. Of course, since you are just catching it rather than stealing it, your Victim has to cooperate with you to the extent of not catching that ball. He also has to know in advance what you are going to do. The act of standing behind him can be his signal. To someone watching from out front, the balls are going in exactly the same pattern they would go if one person were doing a Regular Cascade.

Overhead Take-Away: Closely related to this is the Overhead Take-Away. Your Victim should be quite a bit shorter than you. Stand behind him, and reach over his shoulders to take away the balls. By bending his knees, he can carefully duck down and crawl out from under your hands. Reverse this by having him return to his position while you drop the balls down to him. See the next section on Drop-Downs.

GIVE-AWAYS

Drop-Downs. There are many ways that one juggler can give the balls to another. The "Drop-Down" is a simple move in which one juggler stands very close to the other, facing him but much lower. The usual position is for the Receiver to be crouched or kneeling on the floor or for the Giver to be standing on a chair or platform, or simply to be much taller than the Receiver. The Giver simply lets the balls fall by not catching them, and the Receiver catches them and juggles. The balls move as they do in the Face-to-Face (right-left-right). The ball coming from the Giver's right hand goes across and lands in the Receiver's right hand, and vice versa.

Quick and Slow Succession. There are two basic ways of doing a ball transfer: Quick Succession and Slow Succession. When the balls are transferred right-left-right, as in the Take-Aways, this is a "Quick-Succession Transfer." If you transfer all the balls with the same hand, right-right-right, it takes longer; this is a "Slow-Succession Transfer." The rhythm for the Quick Succession is RIGHT-LEFT-RIGHT, while the corresponding rhythm for the Slow Succession is RIGHT-Left-RIGHT-Left-RIGHT, taking almost twice as long to get all three balls transferred.

Drop-Ups. A "Drop-Up" is the reverse of a Drop-Down. The lower juggler is now the Giver, throwing high throws that the other person intercepts as in a Take-Away. The difference between this and a Take-Away is that in Drop-Ups the Giver is purposely throwing the balls up out of his normal pattern to someone else. The Drop-Up can be a Quick- or Slow-Succession Transfer. These two variations, the Drop-Down and the Drop-Up, can alternate with each other, as do the Take-

60

Aways.

Other Give-Aways. There are many other possible Give-Aways, such as Bouncing Give-Aways, Side-by-Side Passing, or Partial Passing, in addition to the Drop-Backs and Face-to-Face Partial Passing mentioned before. There are also Bouncing Take-Aways, a variation that my students researched and worked up into a performable routine, doing a really fine job.

This concludes Part II on the exploration and refinement of the major variations of three-ball juggling and passing. You should continue to work on these things, and explore new areas. Do not close off any possibilities. I can hardly give you one-tenth of all the possible avenues of development in the Juggler's Art. You will know what you have a taste for, and you should go after that. This book is only to get you started and to give you some hints. The rest is up to you.

Further Ball Work. Later in this book, there will be some advanced ball work: Two-Ball Juggling, the One-and-One, the Two-and-One, and Four- and Five-Ball Juggling. These are placed at the end of the book, and should be left for later. In the meantime go on to club and hoop juggling. Advanced Two-, Four-, and Five-Ball Juggling work involves different rhythms and different energy patterns and requires a lot of relearning. I think it is better to continue as long as possible with the basic three-object rhythm pattern to which you have become accustomed. You can use the energy you have already built up to propel you into learning clubs and hoops much faster than if you broke off now and tried to return to it later. Also, since almost all of the ball variations have their counterparts in clubs, you should work on clubs as soon as possible after learning balls.

III.
Club
&
Hoop
Juggling

Lesson 17: Basic Club Juggling

You are now about to enter into a new level of juggling—club juggling. Be prepared for a possible but temporary setback as you start working with new equipment and using new muscles. Never be satisfied with one level of proficiency, saying, "Well, I am a juggler now, since I can do this and that." There is no end to this study. It is a continuing process of growing and building that should never end and should never become tiresome or boring.

In this part of the book, I am not going to give you quite as much in the way of detailed instruction as I did in the work on ball juggling. For one thing, having worked through that material, you are a different person than you were when you began. You are something of a juggler by now. Your club juggling will be based on your ball juggling; how fast and how well you learn will generally depend on how well you have worked with balls. Some people prefer to work with balls, while others find clubs easier.

By now, you are also more familiar with *how* you learned to juggle, and you will be able to map out your own exercises and practices to a much greater extent. Also, it is more difficult to give a complete description of every detail of club juggling, such as the positions of the club as it turns. This is because of the complex interrelationship between the height of the throw, the amount of turning, wrist and arm action, and the residual energies in your body.

Equipment. The very first order of business in club juggling is to get some clubs to work with. Unless the popularity of juggling increases dramatically in this country, there will be no such thing as clubs that you can buy in a store. You will have to make your own. This is not as hard as you might think. Just go to your local laundromat and find three white plastic clorox bleach bottles (or some other brand, as long as the bottles are round, and all of the same kind). Also, find two discarded handles from sponge-type mops. These handles are thinner than regular broomsticks and fit very snugly into the bleach bottles. The important thing is a tight fit. Then go to a medical supply house and get three crutch tips that just fit over the ends of the mop handles. Finally, you will need a few long carpet tacks, or large-headed nails, and a hammer, a saw, and a pocketknife. You now have everything you need to make a set of perfectly balanced juggling clubs.

Cut the mop handles into three pieces, each eighteen inches long, cutting the ends off evenly. Then soak one end of each handle for a short time in hot, soapy water, or put soap on the handles. You may have to whittle the ends of the handles a little to force them into the openings of the bleach bottles. Stand the handle on a workbench or a surface you don't care about, and fit the bottle on the upper end of it. By lifting the bottle and handle together, slamming them down together on the workbench, and exerting a lot of force on the neck of the bottle, the handle should go in. You can't push too hard on the bottle itself without crushing it, so just pull the neck of the bottle down over the stick. If the fit is not 100 percent tight, you will have to use some small tacks around the neck of the bottle to keep the club from coming loose as you use it.

Push the handle on into the bottle until it makes contact with the bottom. When you are sure that it is in the exact center of the bottom by tapping around and feeling for it, drive in a long nail or tack to hold it. Put a crutch tip on the other end of the handle, and you are in business!

If, after some use, the bottle loosens up or the neck splits, use small carpet tacks to hold it together. By selecting handles of different colors, you will have a set of marked clubs, which will be useful in the lessons to follow, as the marked balls were previously. As a final touch, you can cover these handles with some clear celluloid.

For a somewhat heavier, more professional set of clubs, buy a set of ten large-size plastic bowling pins from your local toy store Saw the tops off just above the narrowest point. Then buy some 1 1/8-inch-wide dowels in a lumberyard, and cut pieces eighteen

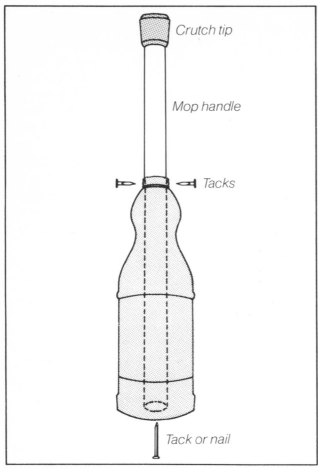

Crutch tip

Mop handle

Tacks

Tack or nail

De Luxe juggling club made from bleach bottle and mop handle

inches long. Take the cut bowling pins along with you to the lumberyard to be sure you are getting dowels of the right size. Slide these in and nail the ends as described for the bleach bottles. You are probably going to have to split the neck on opposite sides and overlap the pieces as you tack them down. To mark it put colored tape over the tacks around the neck and a strip around the center of the head of the club. Get your pocketknife out and whittle the handle. Taper it down from the neck, so that it fits nicely in your hand. Leave the last inch untouched to make a knob. With knife and sandpaper, smooth this knob all around. Also sandpaper the handle.

As an added feature for these clubs, buy some heavy theater gel or the heavy plastic or celluloid used to cover desk blotters, which can be bought at large stationery stores. Cut a piece that can be shaped around the handle. It should extend from the base of the knob up to a point about a quarter-inch beyond the tacked area. The main thing is to have a hollow space under the plastic. This allows the handle to give as you catch the club, which will make it a lot easier on your hands. Wrap the plastic around the handle twice, and tape it down at both ends and along the exposed edge. For about eight dollars, you will have

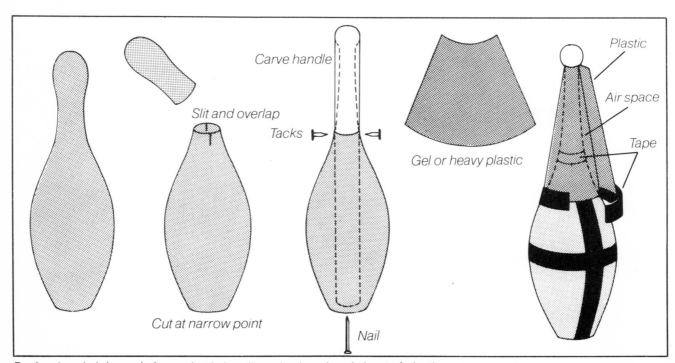

Carve handle

Slit and overlap

Tacks

Cut at narrow point

Nail

Gel or heavy plastic

Plastic

Air space

Tape

Professional club made from plastic bowling pin, dowel and sheet of plastic

a set of ten clubs very close in quality to those used by many professional jugglers.

Right now you only need to make three clubs, unless you want to provide for your partner at the same time. The clubs should be as much alike as you can make them, which is important for passing. These clubs should last you quite a while. Later, after you have fully mastered the Club Cascade and Club Throws, you can consider using brushes, small brooms, pots, sticks, mailing tubes, plastic bats, nightsticks, and even, if you insist, knives and torches. Until you are well seasoned avoid very heavy "real" objects such as Indian clubs and bowling pins, which can be very dangerous.

Holding. The first thing to learn is how to throw a club to yourself and catch it properly. Take one of the clubs you have just made and hold it in your right hand. Lay the club across your hand so your thumb is on one side of the club and the rest of your fingers are on the other side. Your hand should be in the center of the handle, not touching either the head of the club or the knob. In Home Position, the head of the club in your right hand will naturally point out to the right at a 45-degree angle. To simplify the description, I will be referring to a direction along a diagonal as toward the right-hand or left-hand *corner*.

Holding a club

Throwing. Now move the club around so that it points to the left-hand corner. Do this by dropping it down and scooping it around in a little arc, so that when it points to the left-hand corner it is on the way upward. The arc is down, around, and up, just like the egg-beater hand-motion in ball juggling. Let the club continue on upward, with your wrist doing all the work, not your arm. Before you throw the club again, you must swing it down, around, and up, so it points to the right-hand corner before it leaves your hand again. Every time you throw it, you have to aim it in the new direction first. It will be making a kind of figure eight or infinity sign as it goes from hand to hand. After a while you will begin to feel the rhythm and the flow of this motion.

Height. Make your throws to the same height as much as possible. The minute you throw a club up to a different height, you change the timing and with it the amount of turning, even if you don't change the force given to the club by your wrist. If you throw the club too low, you will have less time, and you will have to turn the club faster to get it all the way around before it lands. If you throw the club too high, you will have more time, and you will have to turn it slower to prevent it from going around more than once. This is contrary to the natural inclination to add energy all over, making the club turn more as you throw higher. It will spin around like crazy, and you'll never catch it. In the beginning, it is best to keep the clubs about a foot above your head. Later on, the height will gradually drop, as it did with the balls, until you can see over the tops of the clubs.

Catching. The natural position of your catching hand will allow the club, if it is thrown correctly, to fall directly between your thumb and fingers, the head pointing to the corner on the side on which it is caught. Your hands will stay in Home Position as you catch the club. Avoid having your hands come close to each other. You should maintain the same open space in front of your stomach that you did in ball juggling. Also, don't let the clubs point straight ahead, parallel to each other. They are always thrown across your body from one side to the other, so that the pattern is almost flat against you.

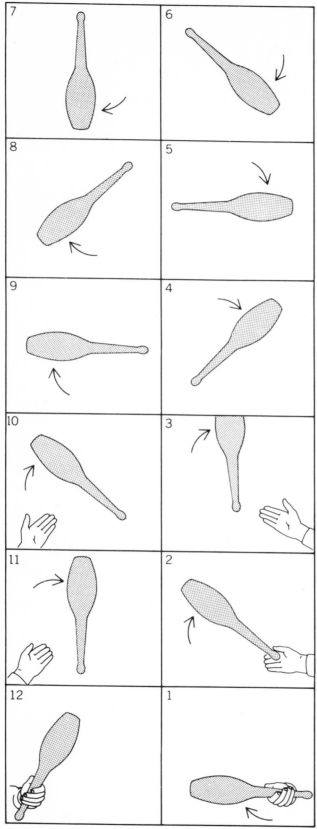

Club Passing. Position of the club as it passes through the air

Turning. If a club is not turned correctly, it is called either overturned or underturned. You can tell how much a given club is overturned or underturned by where you actually catch it. If your hand has to go up to catch a club, way above the Tray Plane, then that club is overturned. You are instinctively going up there to catch it before it has turned too much. If, however, your hand is going down below the Tray Plane to catch a club, or if you are bending down so that you are catching it around your knees or close to the ground, these are signs that you are underturning the club. You are instinctively going down to wait for the club to come around properly.

Avoid throwing the club and catching it with the same hand. Keep working until you can throw every club to the same height and have the club turn the same amount each time—neither overturned nor underturned.

One Club, Two Balls. When you are satisfied with your "Basic Club Throw," start on this section. Put one club in your right hand and the two balls in your left. Start juggling by throwing one of the balls from your left hand. Then throw the club and you are off into Cascade juggling with mixed objects. Practice starting with the lone club in each of the other two possible places in your hands. In the beginning you might practice the Cascade Progression, working through one throw, two throws, three throws, and so on, as you did in ball juggling. The main problem you will have on ending is catching a ball when you already have a club in your hand, or the other way around. You will have to judge how you can go about solving this.

As you do this mixed juggling, remember all the things I told you about swinging the club down, around, and up before throwing it, so that it points to the opposite corner. The more to the side, rather than out front, that these corners are, the better. This will keep the clubs closer to your body in a kind of flat pattern, and it will look clear and clean to someone standing in front of you. This will be easier to maintain as you go on with it. In time, your pattern will be wide and low, so the people watching can see what you are doing, and you can see who's watching you. Keep working on this until you feel the club fitting in smoothly with the balls.

Vamping. Just as you learned to Vamp two balls, you should now work on Vamping two clubs. Hold one club in each hand, with a red club in your right. Throw the red club in your right hand across to your left. Your left hand will come up slightly, and open. The club in your left hand will move out, and this hand will move to the outside just in time to catch the turning handle of the incoming club. Again, it is very important to throw wide, so that there is ample room for the two clubs to get past one another. It is extremely difficult to convey in words, or even in pictures, the precise nature of this "Club Exchange." It is an organic thing happening in time, and it is not too readily captured to be looked at analytically. Some things are easier said (done) than done (said).

Practice this Vamping, throwing the red club from your right hand, followed immediately by the other club from your left hand. Then throw the red club from your left hand first, followed immediately by the other from your right hand. Between each pair of throws is a single beat where the missing club would have been thrown. This Vamping is basically no different from juggling with three clubs, except for this phantom club. It gives you a little time between Vamps to reset yourself.

Two Clubs, One Ball. Add a single ball to the two clubs you have just been Vamping. Put the ball in your left hand and the two clubs in your right. You do this by picking up one club in the normal way with your right hand. Then, turn that hand over, palm up. Place the second club on top of the first so they make an X. This second club goes between your index finger and your middle finger. Make sure that you have a good hold on both clubs, without clutching them excessively, which makes it hard to let go of them.

Then lower your right hand to your side for a moment in such a way that this second club is lined-up forward and back. Then bring that hand back up to Home Position. The second club that you put in your hand is the first one that you throw. Move your wrist up and down a few times until you get the feeling that this club to be thrown is really the only thing in your hand. Then throw it. You will have to pull the other club up out of the way quickly as you let this one fly. Otherwise, the

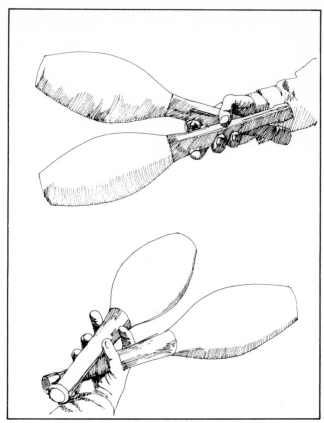

How to hold two clubs

handles may get in each other's way, and the thrown club may go off in some other direction. Once you get the feel of it, the throwing of the first club ceases to be a problem.

You can also try variations where the two clubs occupy the other two possible combinations of starting positions. The main purpose of this exercise is to practice throwing the first club when you have another one in that hand. Once you have this, you should move right along to three clubs.

Three Clubs. You now have all the parts you need in order to do three clubs. Start with two clubs in your right hand, as above, and one in your left. Once you get the first club launched properly, all you have to think about is doing the Club Exchanges alternately in your right and left hands. All the old bugaboos will be there again: throwing out forward, or too narrow, or to all different heights, and collisions and drift. In addition, you will be contending with a new bugaboo: getting the clubs to turn the right amount on each throw.

Simple Ending. In order for you to have a nice unit of work to tackle, you should immediately learn a club ending. In this simple ending you do something similar to the reverse of what you did when you threw the club: Turn your hand palm-up, stick your fingers out, and grab the club last as it lands between your index and middle fingers. The two handles will hit together with a resounding clunk, and your clubs will be in the same position they were in when you started the volley. This is actually easier than it sounds. But if you can't get it, you can always just let the third club drop when you want to stop, or wait until you miss.

Three-Clubs Practice. You have all the techniques that you were given in the earlier part of this book to guide you. The Home Position and Freeze are still useful. Remember especially not to let your arms fly up and down, a particular temptation when doing clubs. Instead, keep your energy concentrated in your hands and wrists. Club juggling will put a maximum strain on your wrists, but after a week or so you will find them getting stronger. Someday you will be able to juggle three-pound bowling pins with (ease?).

Lesson 18: Advanced Club Work

After you have become pretty confident with clubs in the Regular Cascade, you should take your club juggling through all the steps you went through with ball juggling. Since these exercises were covered thoroughly in the first part of this book, I won't go over them again here. Club equivalents include juggling to rhythm, juggling before a mirror, watching the shadows of the objects, squinting and blind juggling, sitting, kneeling, sitting on the floor, lying down, and juggling in combination with various body movements. Refer back to the appropriate lessons to refresh your memory.

This lesson will cover the club equivalents of material given you in Lessons 7 through 11.

They include explorations in Pattern Size; Reverse Cascade; Downward, Upward, and Sideways Clawing; and various Body Throws (Behind-the-Back, Over-the-Shoulder, Under-the-Wrist, and Cross-Handed). Of course the lesson on Bouncing (Lesson 12) has no counterpart in clubs, aside from an exotic area where you slap the clubs in mid-air, making them spin around in different ways.

Pattern Size. As you explore the Pattern Sizes, you may have trouble attempting to juggle wide. One way to help yourself here is to be sure always to point the club in the direction toward which you are going to throw it. The moment a club leaves your hand, it will continue to point in exactly that same direction until you catch it again. If you don't point it in the direction you are throwing it, it will go sideways, sort of like a boomerang or a propeller going through the air. This will make it difficult or impossible to catch.

"Narrow Pattern" means that the clubs are almost parallel to each other. (Beginning club jugglers have this tendency.) "Wide Pattern" means that your clubs are just about parallel to your chest and close to it as they go across.

Reverse Cascade. If you practice doing a Reverse Cascade in strict rhythm, just the way you were doing it with balls, you will soon find that the handle of the club just thrown will almost always hit, knob for knob, the handle of the club coming in. To solve this problem, you have to "cheat" a little. As you throw the club, slip your hand a little forward, also the club to which you are giving an Overthrow. This will bring the two handles out of each other's way. Also, exaggerate the size of the Overthrow, and make this Set-Up throw very short and very low. Try this. Experiment with various ways of throwing the clubs to avoid these collisions. A Full Shower of Overthrown clubs takes some work but looks really fine.

Clawing. As a club in the Regular Cascade comes down into your hand, the handle should be level, pointing to your stomach, and the club should be in the Tray Plane, just as it touches your hand. Now go back to a moment before that. An instant earlier, as the club was moving down to the Tray Plane and your hand, the handle must have been pointing straight up. The trick of Club Clawing is to grab the club at the instant the handle is vertical. The head of the club will be pointing downward, and your hand will come down forcefully along the handle, the way it does when you are clawing a ball. Because you have caught the club before it has come all the way around, it will take less time to turn to this position. The first few times you try it, you will probably have to throw the club higher and slower to get some extra time to see when to claw.

Since it took only three-quarters of a turn to get the club into this handle-up clawing position, it will take one and one-quarter more turns to get it back out into a normal catch. You will have to give the club some extra energy for this. At the same time, your hand will be in an awkward position: Your palm is down, your hand is on top of the handle, which points away from you, while the head of the club is under your forearm. This is the reverse of the normal position. With some work, you can easily do a Full Shower of Club Clawing. Notice that if you claw two in a row with the same hand, the rotation between catches is now back to exactly one full turn.

CLUB CLAWING VARIATIONS

Over-The-Head. Lean back while doing this Full Shower and raise the clubs over your head. The position of your hands on the clubs lends itself to this position. It is a difficult position quite hard to stabilize, since there is a strong tendency for the clubs to continue on back and fall behind you. The only way you can keep going is to move back to catch them. Try to keep them in one place once you get them up there. At first, go up a short distance and come back down. Later, go higher and higher. Always recover before you miss. Recovery is necessary after every variation.

Upward and Sideways. Upward Clawing for clubs is very similar to that described for balls. The Exchange is very short and late. You might find that the extra energy generated by

the late catch will send the club up into a Double. This is fine once you have learned how to handle Doubles. But you should be throwing a Single or a Double because you are in control, not just accidentally.

To prepare for Sideways Clawing, reach out your right hand as you would for regular Club Clawing. Then rotate it exactly half a turn counterclockwise. Your thumb should be below your hand, pointing downward and out, and your fingers above. Your elbow will be sticking out. As a club comes around, reach to the inside of the handle and claw it sideways to the right. Then bring it around in a quick sweep, ready to throw again.

Behind-The-Back. It is a rule that the closer to the knob you hold a club when throwing it, the slower it will turn and the higher it will go. This principle is used with the Behind-the-Back and other Body Throws. In Behind-the-Back, the clubs are thrown from a level below the Tray Plane. You also have to throw the club higher to clear your shoulder. To get this slower motion more easily, let the club slide down so the knob is in your hand just before throwing it. This will keep the club from going around twice.

Under-the-Leg throws can also be improved by throwing from the knob. The Under-the-Wrist throw mentioned in ball juggling is especially nice with clubs, and it creates the effect of an almost impossible maneuver, with clubs and hands flying all about in a blur. In another variation, called "Reversed Clubs," you hold the clubs by the heads rather than the handles. You do half-turns or one-and-a-half turns to change from handle to head or back. With juggling sticks, or any object that has both ends the same, you can turn the object any number of half-turns.

This lesson has been a collection of miscellaneous comments on certain club variations that are different from their ball equivalents. Try these out, and then go on to the next lesson on Throws and Endings. Later, when you are able to throw Doubles and nice Endings you should return to this lesson to develop the material here more fully.

Lesson 19: Club Throws, Beginnings & Endings

The term "Club Throw" refers to Doubles, Triples, Spins (an indefinite number of turns), Flats (no turns), and Reverses (one turn the other way). There are also Double Reverses, Half-Turns, the Side Overthrow, and the Long-Sideways Double.

Club Beginnings and Endings depend upon your ability to do good Club Throws.

CLUB THROWS

Doubles. It goes without saying that you should have your regular club juggling perfected before working on "Doubles." Doubles liberate a lot of energy, and this is one of the main problems in dealing with them.

The Double is a double turn of the club while it is in the air. It is done by adding an extra amount of energy in your wrist as you throw, increasing both the rotation and the height of the club. A Double should be thrown higher than a Single, especially in the beginning, since the extra height will give the club more time to turn. Your Singles, by this time, are probably down close to eye-level or below. Start your Doubles where your Singles started, about a foot above your head. In club juggling, at this point in your development, there are two levels of energy: that for the Single and that for the Double. There is nothing in between. If you are juggling clubs and you want to throw a Double, you have to deliver the exact amount of extra energy. There can be no guessing, sliding up to it, or tuning into it later. It has to be right. If you use an amount of energy that is in between, the club may go around one and one-half times or so, and you will find yourself trying to catch it by the head rather than by the handle.

One problem often encountered with Doubles is the tremendous build-up of energy that occurs as you do larger and larger numbers of these throws. You must keep a constant watch to prevent this from happening. Let the energy go away after each volley, and even after each throw. When you let yourself become excited or carried away you will find yourself letting this excess energy get into your throws. You may find yourself out of control, throwing Triples or Spins, or at least overturning the Doubles, and you will have a harder time catching them. Keep your center: Don't let outside or inside energy get into the wrong places; don't get excited. You should plan your work with regard to the energies involved. It is not good to do extremely low-energy juggling right after high-energy work. There will be too much carry-over, and you won't be able to tune in to the subtlety and fine adjustment of the low-energy work. It is best to do all the low-energy things first and work up to the high-energy things later. In terms of performing, this is a generally accepted rule: Save the hard things and the goodies for last.

Full-Shower of Doubles. Using a red club, start by throwing a Double every third time this red club comes around. Increase the frequency of throws until you are throwing a Double on every third club, without regard to color. This is equivalent to throwing a Double on every red club. Proceed with the Full-Shower Progression, delivering more and more Doubles within a given number of throws until you are doing only Doubles — or a Full-Shower of Doubles.

Long-Sideways Doubles. This is a special throw of the Double that has some good performance possibilities. Do regular Cascade club juggling. Then throw one club as a Double, but throw it from your right hand straight across over your left forearm. Make this throw a long one, so the club doesn't complete its double rotation until it gets about two feet past your left arm. Then reach out quickly with your left hand and grab it back in. The effect is better if you don't even look in that direction. If you do this with the red club, it will look as if this club had a mind of its own.

Triples. Generally, the same principles apply to throwing "Triples" as to Doubles — only in spades. Each problem you had with Doubles will be greatly magnified when you start doing

Triples. Do not start Triples, or even experiment with them, until your Doubles are low and stable. When practicing, you should start your volley with Singles, go into a Full-Shower of Doubles, and from there start throwing a Triple or two, eventually working up into all Triples. You will find that a Triple, and even a Double to some extent, is gauged less by the number of turns the club makes than by the time and height intervening between the throw and the catch. From juggling Doubles, throw the Triples a bit higher, and stick your hand out at exactly the right moment. The handle should be there if you have increased the height just right and waited just the right length of time. In the beginning, you might have to search around for the handle—dropping below the Tray Plane if the club is underturned, or going up above it if the club is overturned. Later, you will be able to put your hand out and a club will always be there.

If you have constructed your clubs properly, the handle will stick out further than the head as it turns in the air. So to some extent, you can hold your hand out and wait for the handle. Don't rely on this to save you any work, though. You can only fake so much, and juggling is the wrong field for fakers.

After you can do a Full-Shower of Triples, try to bring them down as you did the Singles and Doubles. By the time you get them down in front of your face, they are nothing but a blur. You don't even think of them as clubs any more. The whole operation is now governed by time and rhythm. With Doubles especially, it is fairly easy to get to the place where you can look around the room while juggling.

Quadruples are possible, but once you go beyond Triples you start to lose the definition of what you are doing—that is, people cannot distinguish between Triples and Quadruples. Therefore, if you want to be a "juggler's juggler," you can get into this and many more variations which will get you some respect from your fellow hurlers-of-objects.

Recovery. Recovery from Doubles, and especially from Triples, is a problem. Once you have built your energy up to that level, it is a very hard thing to bring it down smoothly. You will have to really pull back on your Triples, until it hardly feels like you are turning the clubs. If you pull back on three clubs in a row in Quick Succession (right, left, right), you can get back to Doubles. With another such pulling back, so that you make absolutely no effort at all to turn the clubs, you can get back to Singles. Another way out of Triples is to do an Ending, which I will cover in the last part of this lesson.

Flats. A "Flat" is a Club Throw in which the club does not turn at all. It just goes up in the air as though suspended, like the ball that does not spin. To do Flats, start with Singles. Then, as you throw a club, quickly slide your hand toward yourself, along the handle toward the knob, keeping it in contact with the handle. As you do this, the handle will start to rise, and you will have to follow it with your hand in order to keep contact. It might be better to say that you slide your hand more in an upward direction.

Since a normal throw makes the *head* of the club go upward and therefore turns the club in the air, the pushing of the *handle* upward has the effect of making the handle catch up with the head. If you impart the right amount of force, it nullifies the turning that the club would ordinarily do, and the club goes up flat. The only problem is that the upward push on the handle has to exactly match the upward motion of the head. If it is more, the handle will gain on the head. If it is less, the club will just be turning slower, and it may go into a position that makes it hard to catch. Another problem is that the handle sometimes gets pushed sideways as it goes up, causing the club to be rotated in a horizontal plane like a propeller beanie. It may be pointing in another direction entirely by the time it comes down. It is possible to get the club to rotate just once in this flat plane before it comes down, which adds to the effect.

A Full-Shower of Flats is easy to learn Your wrist and hand move in a direction opposite to the normal way, with your fingers trailing up the handle. Because of this, and because of the lower energy required, it is best not to do Flats just after you have done Doubles or Triples.

Reverses. Once you can do Flats, push still harder on the handles so that they now gain on the heads. This will make the club go around in the opposite direction. As the club is ready to be caught, the handle will be coming up from below to the Tray Plane, rather than coming down from above as usual. To catch this, simply turn your hand palm-down, grab the club, and then turn your hand back over again in time to make the next throw. A "Reverse" is a little like a ball-clawing catch. Double Reverses are also possible for the advanced juggler, but they require an enormous amount of energy and control.

Sideways Overthrow. Bring your right hand and its club-about-to-be-thrown straight out to the right side of your body, and throw a high Double back in over your own head to your left side. As you are about to catch it, the handle of the club will be coming down at you from above, and will be pointing toward the outside of your body (to your left). Reach up and catch it while it is in this position and about a foot above your head. You will be catching it with your left hand in the same position you would use to hang from a branch, palm forward. The club will be very hard to catch if it goes beyond that point. Experiment with various throws to get the club just to this place. These "passover" throws are pretty, especially if you do a Half-Shower of them over your head. I have never seen a Full-Shower of them, but then one purpose of this book is to inspire you to go beyond what has already been done. In a Full-Shower, the collision problem might be a major one and kind of disastrous unless you wear a helmet.

CLUB BEGINNINGS

Two Club Beginning. Throw both clubs in your right hand up at the same time. As they come down, reach in under them and with your left hand give the third club a Double so that it goes out ahead of the other two and has room to turn. Then catch the first two clubs, one in each hand, and go after the Double. Throw the club in your right hand up under the Double as it comes down, and go into juggling. After you have worked on this for a while, you will be ready for that show-stopper, the Three-Club Beginning.

Three Club Beginning. Grasp all three clubs in a bunch in your right hand. Your hand should be at about the centers of the handles. Then pull the center club out away from you, so that only the knob remains in your hand. Let that club hang down below the other two, at an angle. The other two clubs should be arranged side by side. When you throw all three at the same time, the club that was pulled out will go higher than the other two (just as the ball in the Three-Ball Beginning did because it was on your fingertips). It will also go around twice, because it has more time to turn. Catch the first two normally, one in each hand, as in the Two Club Beginning. Then as the third club finally comes down after its Double, begin juggling. You will have to reach forward for this third club, depending on how far away you threw it.

Outside Foot Kick-Up Beginning. Place the neck of the club across the instep of your right foot so that the head of the club points straight out to the right. Flex your foot so your toes are raised to form a cradle for the handle. As much of the handle as possible should be to the inside of your foot. Then step as far forward as you can with your left foot, so that the club is directly under your right hip, keeping the toes of your right foot raised a little. This will mean that your calf, or shin bone, is angled forward, making an acute angle with your right foot, and the handle (or better, the neck) of the club is lying in this angle or hook.

Then quickly draw your foot up under you. Don't kick forward, but raise your knee, bringing your heel up to your rear end. If you have done this properly, the neck of the club will get caught in that angle, causing the head to continue on up. The club will turn once, and the handle will come around to your right hand just at the Tray Plane level. It is easier to do this variation barefooted, since you can get a much better hook around the handle of the club. I can't imagine what it would be like to juggle with my shoes on.

CLUB ENDINGS

High-Throw Ending. This is the same basic ending as the High-Throw Ending you did with the balls. Throw one slow Double up with your right hand, making sure that it is slightly underturned. While it is out of your hand, transfer the next club in your right hand across to your left by bringing your hands together temporarily. Now your right hand is free to catch the Double as it comes down. The value of this is that, since there is no other club in your right hand, there is almost no chance of missing this final, crucial catch.

Spin Ending. As you did with balls, you can spin yourself around using the momentum of your arm after you make the last catch. It feels right when you do it, and it is a neat wrap-up of the energy you are putting out.

Run Ending. By throwing a "Club Spin" up and forward, you have the opportunity to run after it and catch it. Don't forget to make the transfer in your hands as you run. You will have plenty of chance to grab the last club at the right place in its turning—if it hasn't turned enough, you can just stay with it and catch it near the ground when it has turned enough. This ending rarely fails. It is a snappy performance ending that has such flair it almost forces people to applaud, regardless of what you did before.

High Flat Ending. This ending is similar to the High Throw, except that the club is thrown flat. Throw it nice and high. This is especially impressive if you have just been doing Triples, and out of that whirlwind sails one perfectly flat club.

Lesson 20: Club Passing

Before you start to think about passing clubs, you must first have your regular club juggling under perfect control, as I have said many times before. Second, you must have a partner with whom you have worked and have done all the *ball* passing and other material for partners; a partner with whom you work extremely well, and whose skill is just about equal to yours.

Throwing. Passing involves a new way to throw a club. The throw is a forward one, not across to your other hand, but straight out in front of your right hand. This is exactly what you had to learn *not* to do when you first juggled balls. Note that there is no such thing at this level of the work as a diagonal throw to your partner. The throw is across from your own right hand either to your own left hand or to your partner's left hand. These are the Selfs and Passes that you learned in the lesson on ball passing.

When you throw a ball upward, as in the Regular Cascade, you have a level plane, the Tray Plane, from which to start. The difference between ball and club passing is that the club must be thrown almost straight across on a level line, while the ball is thrown almost vertically in a high arc. Every throw in juggling, whether ball or club, comes from your hand at approximately right angles to your forearm. Therefore to throw a club straight across, your forearm must be vertical, *not* horizontal. To do this, you should be throwing from a vertical plane, parallel to the Wall Plane and passing through your body.

Throwing Practice. These instructions will be given from the standpoint of throwing from your right hand and catching with your left. Some variations are possible where the throw is from your left hand, or from both hands at the same time. Later, you should work on passing from your left hand as well.

Stand about eight or ten feet from your partner. Swing the club down beside your leg to a point about six to eight inches behind your leg and right next to it. As the club approaches this point, imagine that you are pushing back against a spring, that you are meeting some resistance to moving your hand and arm back there. Then, yield to this resistance and let it push your arm immediately forward. As your arm starts to come up past your leg, let go of the club. The exact point of release is different for every person. It depends on how far back you took the club, how fast you came forward with it, and what amount of wrist action you are imparting to it if any. If the club flies too high, release it sooner. If it goes too low, hang onto it a little longer. There should be very little deliberate wrist action to make the club turn, since the motion of your arm does that automatically. Keep the club swing in a vertical plane as you throw, or you will get a kind of wobbling effect and the club will be very hard to catch.

Path. The club will leave your hand in line with your arm. According to just where your hand released it, the handle of the club should be pointing up and toward your right arm. As the club starts to travel, the handle begins to rotate downward around the head, the same as if a wheel were rolling *toward* you, in spite of the fact that the club itself is going away from you. As the head comes up, the handle goes down. The handle continues to rotate around to a forward orientation away from you, goes upward, then toward you again after one full rotation, and finally downward again. In the full-throw to your partner, the club rotates almost a turn and a half. By this time it has come to a position with the handle pointing straight down. At this point it should be about a foot in front of your partner's shoulder. If you wish to practice throwing, but you don't always have a partner available, throw toward some cushions propped up against the wall on the back of a sofa or couch. The club should smack into the cushion flat, with the handle down. Practice this until you can do it consistently, having it hit the cushion so the center of the club is level with what would be your partner's shoulder.

Catching. To catch a thrown club, bring your left hand up to shoulder level so that it is just about two inches outside your left shoulder. Before the club arrives, curve your fingers just as if you were grasping a vertical post. As the club comes to you, it will be approaching the handle-down position. You will see the handle coming into view from under the club, and coming toward you. If it is thrown right, the handle of the club should just about land in your hand. If not, you will have to go after it. When you first try to catch a club, there is a tendency to grab the head, since that is about all you can see at the time. Instead, reach under it, and the handle will come out and land in your hand.

Overturning. If your partner puts too much wrist action on the club as he throws it to you, the club will probably be overturned. It will reach the best catchable position too soon, since it is turning too fast. (The best catchable

Correct position for catching a club

position will be somewhere between you and your partner, rather than at your shoulder.) If you wait for the club to come to you, the handle will have turned past the optimal position. The only way to catch such an overturned club is to recognize it as it travels toward you, and reach forward for it.

Underturning. An underturned club will take a longer time to turn to the right position to be caught. By this time, it has gone by your shoulder, and you have to drop your left hand back behind your shoulder to catch it. If you try to catch the club at the normal place, it will not have come around into the proper handle-down position. The handle will still be behind the head, and so you will have nothing to grab, and the club will slide right through your hand like a bar of soap. Unless you drop back and let the underturned club turn some more, there is no way you can catch it.

These are the basics of catching both overturned and underturned throws. Of course, there will be throws so overturned or underturned that you can't rescue them. The general rule is: For overturned clubs, go forward for the catch; for underturned clubs, go backward.

Throwing and Catching Practice. You should work with your partner on both the throw and the catch until you have them really under control. If one of you is much more advanced than the other, you may find that the better juggler is making spectacular saves as he catches the bad throws of the poorer juggler. Thus the poorer juggler never sees just how bad his throws are, since they are always caught. And if the better juggler is always delivering good throws, the poorer juggler never has the experience of trying to catch any bad ones. Then the poorer juggler never learns an important part of the work, and he is deluded into thinking that he is better than he really is.

When you are working with a partner, you should keep a running communication going between you. Each juggler should call out, "overturned," "underturned," "inside," "outside," "high," or "low," as the case may be, so the other person can adjust his throws. Remember this later, when you and your partner are working with six clubs in various complex formations where it is not always possible for you to see where your throws have gone. An important point is to keep your eye on your partner. Make sure he is not throwing another club while you are picking up dropped ones. It is a good safety policy for both jugglers to stop juggling the minute it becomes apparent that either one has missed.

Inside Throws. One special problem in club passing is the "Inside Throw." The club comes close to the face of the receiver, which is not only a dangerous situation but one difficult to deal with and recover from. Most of this comes from the tendency to throw across to your own left hand, making the club end up as a corner throw. Another possible reason for this may be that your Set-Up throw before the pass is not wide enough, causing the club you are passing to be crowded over to your left. This crowding also gives rise to collisions between your own clubs. One clue that you are

throwing inside is if you see your partner continually stepping to *his* right, trying to move over out of the way. A surer clue is if you see your partner ducking his head, and hollering.

Lofting. A convention among club jugglers defines the way to return a club that was dropped to another juggler. Do not throw it to him with a spin, but rather "loft" it. You do this by holding the club in the middle and throwing it so that it remains suspended in the air, making it easier for the other juggler to catch it. It should not be turned since this would put it outside of any variation you are doing, and neither of you is geared for catching it.

Club-Passing Practice. I will not take the space to review here the entire detailed path to learning to pass clubs. Once you have thoroughly perfected your throws and catches with your partner, you should both review the lesson on ball passing. Then start doing all the same things with the clubs. Do the Tuning-In exercise; work on the Throw-In; then the Throw-Out. Bring them together in the Throw-In-and-Out. Go on to Half-Passing, and then Full-Passing. Practice starting together. Then pass Every Third, then every other, then Twosies and Showering, and finally the Three-Three-Ten. Work up to the Three-Three-Ten in the stages outlined. If you covered this territory carefully when you worked on ball passing, you should have very little trouble adapting to club passing.

One way to bridge the gap between balls and clubs is always to start each practice session with ball juggling as a warm up. Whatever pattern you intend to do with clubs, rehearse first with balls. After you have become tuned in to the rhythm and pattern, pick up the clubs and do the same variation.

ADVANCED CLUB TRANSFERS

Side-By-Side Take-Away. A problem exists with this variation that has no equivalent in ball juggling. In a Take-Away with balls, you can snatch them from your Victim and bring them in to yourself. But clubs are larger and heavier, and it is not so easy to snatch them. Also, because of the rotational momentum of the clubs, they tend to act like gyroscopes and do not like to have their direction changed. Therefore, *you* must come to *them.* This means that in a club Take-Away, you have to step into the space in front of your Victim and gently push him back out of the way.

Drop-Back Give-Away. As you did with Drop-Backs in ball juggling, bring the club, you are going to pass up across your chest and let go of it as it goes back over your left shoulder. Here the less you do to it, the better it will go. You will have to rely entirely on your partner to direct you and tell you where to throw so he can catch easily. Again, you have a choice between passing to him in Quick Succession (right-left-right), or in Slow Succession (right-right-right). After he has caught the third club and has gone into a Regular Cascade, you can go around behind him and receive the clubs.

You and your partner can also pass clubs standing back-to-back.

Drop-Forward. The opposite of the Drop-Back is the "Drop-Forward." Here, you throw the clubs forward over your partner's shoulders, while he is facing away from you. *Be careful not to hit him on the head!* Throw a club from your right hand over his left shoulder. Your throw can be fairly wide, and it should also be high enough that he can have some warning about where it is coming down. After you have worked together a lot, you will each develop a feeling about the other's juggling and you will know instinctively where the clubs will be.

Advanced Formations. All the various formations that I outlined in ball passing are possible with clubs. They are the "Cage," the "Shooting Gallery" (be careful in both of these, for clubs hurt more than balls), the "Box," the "Feed," the "Triangle," "Line Passing," "Partial Passing," and the "Run-Around." There is no need for me to go over each of these again here.

This concludes the section on club juggling. Later I will discuss Two-and-One, Two-Ball, Four-Ball, and Five-Ball juggling. Each of these has its counterpart in clubs. I will leave it to you to make the necessary jump from the instructions given for balls to what you will be doing with clubs. There is an enormous number of possible directions for you to go in your juggling, especially club juggling.

Lesson 21: Hoop Juggling

The hoop is the third and last major shape that I will cover in this book. The ball is an object that has all three of its dimensions small and equal. The club has one long dimension, the other two being small and equal. The hoop has only one small dimension, its thickness, while the other two dimensions are large and equal. This then completes the three possible shapes.

Equipment. There are a number of ways to make objects of this general shape. The easiest is to go to a toy store and buy a set of those plastic hoses that you swing around your head to make a kind of whistling, humming sound. Make sure you get the kind that allows you to connect the ends to make a circle. Three of these will give you a set of hoops, ready-made. While they are quite light, they are good enough for learning the basics.

Other materials from which you can make hoops include plywood and plexiglas. The outside diameter should be twelve to fourteen inches, while the rim of the hoop should be about two-and-a-half inches, small enough to allow you to grasp it easily. Don't use material that is so thin it stings your hand when you catch the hoop. One-quarter to three-eighths of an inch is good. You should round the edges both inside and outside with sandpaper to make catching easier. You can also wrap the hoop with tape.

Plates are like hoops in some respects, but you have to grasp them in your hand with your fingers flat on them, which in the beginning can create some difficulty in catching them. Frisbies can also be juggled and have other properties that make for lively performing. Hats, Hula Hoops, and many other round objects are suitable for juggling.

Throwing and Catching. The number of variations possible with hoops, when compared with balls and clubs, is severely limited. For this reason, and because they are very easy to juggle, hoops lend themselves to the "Numbers Game"—that is, juggling increasingly larger numbers of them, up to ten or eleven. Hoops can be thrown very high, they are light, they are stable in orbit, and they are easy to catch. This is because there is no handle to worry about; they are *all* handle. The action of hoops is BIG; therefore, the subtle variations possible with balls, and even clubs, are lost with hoops because of their large size and the greater height to which they have to be thrown.

To throw a hoop, hold it in your hand in a claw position with your palm down. Bring your hand up to your right shoulder, and let go of the hoop with a snap of the wrist, causing it to spin. At the moment of release, the hoop is directly above your hand, at your shoulder. The spin creates a stability in flight, like the spin imparted to a rifle bullet as it goes through the barrel. The hoop is both thrown and caught at your shoulder, close to your body. In hoop juggling there is no Home Position as you have known it.

Catching involves bringing your hand up under the hoop as it comes down, in the same position from which you just threw it. Imagine

Correct position for throwing or catching a hoop

that you were carrying a log on your shoulder—your hand is palm-up. Always catch a hoop at its lowest point. To throw again, bring each hoop down in front of you some distance to get some momentum going. Even so, as in all juggling, try to keep your movements to a minimum.

It is also possible to juggle the hoops from a lower point, down in front of your chest, as you would do with balls or clubs. The catches here are more difficult because you will be catching the hoops by their tops, or at least by the part nearest you. In this position, your hands are palm-down and will be chasing after the hoops as they fall.

Hoop Variations. Variations with hoops are much the same as those you have already done with balls and clubs. They are the Regular Cascade, Rhythm, Mirror, Body Positions, and Body Movements. The Reverse Cascade is possible with hoops, but it is not very noticeable unless you exaggerate it a lot. Also, there are Body Throws, Bouncing off the floor, and Hoop Passing. Passing is similar to and somewhat easier than passing balls or clubs. The hoops are thrown in big, high arcs, with the partners standing further apart than with either balls or clubs. The Two-and-One, to be covered later, is nice with hoops, and you can end your volley by spearing two of the hoops with your hand as they come down together, finishing with a spin and bow.

Sideways Overthrows. Just as with clubs, you can do a nice variation by throwing a hoop up from your right side, over your head and down into your left hand. The advantage of this is that the hoop is flat facing the audience, rather than edge-on. For better visibility, when you do hoops you should stand with your side facing those watching.

Flip-overs. If you have a set of flat hoops, make the two sides of each one different colors. For instance, make one side of each hoop white and the other black. If you stand sideways to the observers, and start with all the white sides showing, you can flip over each hoop in Quick Succession so that they all become black. If you are standing in front of a dark background, they will seem to disappear. You can also make them reappear.

To do a "Flip-over," rotate your right hand counterclockwise, so your elbow comes up and your thumb points outward, just before catching the hoop whose color you want to change. As you turn your hand around to throw it in the regular way, the hoop will be turned over and will change color.

A second way to do this, which is more difficult, is to catch the hoop underhanded and down low in front of you, as in ball juggling. Then turn your hand over in the hoop-throwing position, causing the color to change.

Wrist Spins. Although not strictly juggling, which is defined as throwing and catching more objects than you have hands, this variation is included here to give you a few more things to do with hoops when you are performing. (This variation really belongs in a book on circus arts.) Place one hoop on your right wrist, and move your arm so it spins around clockwise. Now stop, and move it up to your elbow and spin it again. Keep your attention on your elbow, so that it is your elbow that is going up and down in a slight motion. Keep your upper arm out to your right side and your elbow bent at a right angle. While

this is going on, place a second ring on your wrist and send it around in the opposite direction, counterclockwise. To start it off, you will be pushing it downward with your left hand. As you move your arm, you must have your entire forearm, from your elbow to your hand, move up and down exactly parallel. As soon as your hand moves faster or further than your elbow, the hoop on your elbow will stop spinning. If you continue to keep your attention on your elbow and forget about the hoop on your wrist, it will go nicely. The effect of two hoops going in opposite directions on your wrist is pretty. You can do two on each wrist by holding the second ring in your hand, grasping it from the inside.

Mixed Objects. Now that you have become proficient in handling each of the three major categories of objects, the Ball, the Club, and the Hoop, you can combine them, juggling one of each. This is easier than you might think. Each hand will soon learn what object is coming around next, and the hand will be ready to catch and throw it in the particular way that that object requires.

IV.
Advanced
Ball
Juggling

Lesson 22: Two-Ball Juggling

Although it would seem easier to juggle two balls than three, this is not the case, as you shall see. If you divide the number of balls you are juggling by the number of hands you are using, you will get a number called a "Load Factor," which tells you the average number of balls each hand will be able to accommodate. This corresponds roughly to the amount of work each hand is doing. For instance, in the Regular Cascade, three balls divided by two hands gives a Load Factor of 1½ balls per hand. In the work to be covered in this lesson you will have *two* balls in *one* hand. Two divided by one gives a Load Factor of *two* balls per hand. The Load Factor, or work performed by your one hand, in the present two-ball work is greater than either hand in Cascade work. Therefore, in one sense, juggling two balls is harder than three.

The main reason for delaying all the other work with balls (except the Three-Ball Cascade and its variations) until this point in the book is that the rhythm of two-ball juggling is very different from what you have become accustomed to. In three-ball work, the Exchange is very short, and most of the time is waiting time. Here, however, the Exchange occupies almost the full height of the throw, or about half of a full cycle, and the next Exchange begins immediately. At almost every moment some Exchange is going on. Still another difference is that here the balls go more or less straight up and down, rather than across to your other hand.

In the discussion that follows, I am going to assume that you have already become familiar with the first part of this book, can do most of the variations, and are generally aware of the Carlo Method and its terminology. What follows will be a series of exercises to help you adjust to this new pattern and rhythm.

Basic Practice. Stand in Home Position, placing one ball in your right hand. Pop it straight up to eye-level, and let it fall back down into the same hand. Since you are used to throwing the ball at an angle over to your left hand, you should do this exercise until you get used to having the ball come down directly to the same point from which you threw it. Use the Freeze and other Self-Checking techniques that are given throughout this book. Of course, you should work the same way with your left hand, until each hand can do this throw and catch in Home Position without straying.

One Throw. Make a Basket with your right hand and put two balls in it. Throw the fingertip ball up, as you were just doing, and catch it in your same hand. This is similar to the one-throw lesson described earlier. The other ball just sits as a rider in your hand. Try to get every throw to go to the same height. Work on both hands so they get equally strong.

Two Throws. As soon as you start thinking about doing two or more throws from the same hand, you will see that there are two possible paths that the balls can take. These two ways of directing the balls are the Parallel Pattern and the Cyclic Pattern.

Parallel Pattern. In the Many-Throws form of this pattern, you make the first throw, from your fingertips, come down on the right side of your right hand. Throw the second ball straight up from its place. Each ball continues to go up and down in its own column, or "elevator shaft." Your hand simply moves back and forth from the base of one column to the base of the other. You can think of the balls as being thrown from two distinct Tray-Plane points, the Right-Inside and the Right-Outside. Make sure you keep the two columns side by side in the Wall Plane. Don't let them twist around each other in one direction or the other. Especially don't let them get into a forward-and-back orientation to you. You can use this Cascade Progression to build up the length of your volley. Use the Freeze, and check for Spin.

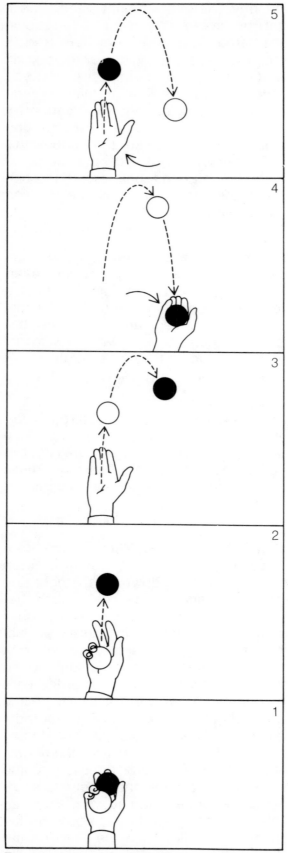

Two-in-one-hand Cyclic Pattern

Cyclic Pattern. The balls can also be directed in such a way that they follow each other around on a cyclic path. As before, throw the first ball from the Basket in your right hand so that it comes down a little to the right of that hand. As it is on the way down, throw the second ball up, but out to the right also, following the first ball. Aim it exactly in the same direction as the first throw so it will come down in the same place that the first ball landed. Catch the first ball, and scoop it down around to the left in a little arc, about five inches across. Throw it up again in a natural continuation of that arc. Each ball will be going up from the left and coming down on the right, each following the other in a kind of flattened vertical ellipse in a clockwise direction. In terms of the Tray Plane, each ball is thrown from the Right-Inside point and is caught at the Right-Outside point.

Inside-Cyclic and Outside-Cyclic Pattern. There are actually two types of Cyclic Pattern. You have just learned the Inside Pattern, which means that the balls go up on the inside and come down on the outside, a little like what your hand would be doing in a Regular Cascade. The Outside Pattern involves sending the balls up on the outside, from the Right-Outside point, and having them come down and be caught at the Right-Inside point. This Outside Pattern has a feeling similar to that of the Overthrow of the Reverse Cascade.

The three basic patterns of Two-Ball work are the Parallel, the Inside-Cyclic, and the Outside-Cyclic. Work on each separately and determine the exact number of throws you want to do before doing them. Work until you develop smoothness, control, and confidence in each hand. Don't forget to make use of the Self-Checking techniques, and also make sure that you give your weaker hand a little extra training. In the Cyclic Patterns especially, there is a tendency for the balls to get into a kind of forward-and-back rolling pattern. Avoid this at all costs. It prevents you from being able to see what you are doing, and anyone watching from the front will be able to see very little of what's going on. As in *all* juggling, the balls should *always* stay in the Wall Plane.

Wide-Parallel Pattern. One nice variation of

the Parallel Pattern is obtained by slowly separating the two columns from each other, getting them as far apart as you can without missing, perhaps several feet. Of course, your hand will have to move from one column to the other, and the wider apart the balls are, the faster your hand is going to have to move. Remember to throw the balls straight up from each point. Always try to make a recovery; just before it is about to blow up, bring your hand slowly back into a Narrow Pattern.

Height. Experiment with various heights. The Parallel Pattern allows you to juggle lower than the Cyclic Patterns, since the balls don't have to go over or around each other. Get the height down to four or five inches, or even less, with your hand moving quickly from one column to the other.

Umbrella and Scoop Movements. You can change from one pattern to the other while juggling by using either the "Umbrella" or the "Scoop" movement. If you are doing the Parallel Pattern and want to go to Inside Pattern, just throw the next ball coming from the Inside point at an angle toward the outside, over the other ball, instead of straight up. The shape of this resembles an umbrella. If you do this with each ball, you will have changed to the Inside Pattern. To get back to the Parallel Pattern, throw one of the balls straight up again from the Inside point. Throw the following ball straight up from the Outside point, and you will be back to Parallel again.

For the Scoop movement you carry the ball from the Inside point to the Outside point (or the reverse) while it is in your hand. Scoop it under the other ball while that one is in the air. If you are doing a Parallel Pattern and want to go to an Inside Pattern, just catch a ball coming down on the outside and scoop it under the other ball, bringing it to the Inside point. Then throw it as described earlier in the section on the Inside-Cyclic Pattern, and continue.

To change directly from the Inside- to the Outside-Cyclic Pattern (or the reverse), you will need two throws. The first throw will take you to the Parallel Pattern, and the second will take you to the reverse cyclic pattern.

Umbrella. This is somewhat similar to the Tennis variation in three-ball work. Here, you are constantly changing from the Outside Pattern to the Inside Pattern and back. Do the two throws to get you one way, and then the two throws to get you to the other. One ball will be going straight up and down over your Right-Center point, in its own column. The other ball will be going back and forth over this one in an Umbrella movement, forming an arc from the Outside point to the Inside point and back.

In slow motion it looks like this: Your hand throws up the first ball at your Right-Center point, and then it goes to the Right-Outside point to throw the second ball from there up and over to the Inside point. Then your hand goes back to the center and again throws the first ball straight up. Then it goes to the Inside point and returns the other ball back to the Outside point. Then your hand goes back to the Center point, and the whole process repeats: center up, outside toward inside, center up, inside toward outside, center up, and so on. The wider you can make this pattern, the more effective it will be.

Scoop. This movement is similar to the Umbrella, except that you Scoop instead. What I call the "Moving Ball," as opposed to the "Center Ball," is scooped from one side to the other, under the Center Ball, rather than being thrown over, as in the Umbrella. The Moving Ball forms a figure shaped like Neptune's trident, the Umbrella figure turned upside-down. Both here and in the Umbrella there are three points in the Tray Plane—inside, center, and outside—involved in the pattern.

Two-Ball Practice. In your practice session, start with your right or better hand and go through One Throw, Two Throws, and so on, building up a smooth volley of throws in each of the three basic variations (Parallel, Inside-Cyclic, and Outside-Cyclic). Extend the Parallel Pattern into the Wide-Parallel Pattern. Experiment with changing from one to the other, and work into the Umbrella and Scoop Movements, letting these become the Umbrella and Scoop variations. Do as much of this sequence of variations as you can without stopping. Then, still without stopping, throw the balls to your other hand, and repeat the whole sequence there. Once you are pretty solid with this, try doing other things with the hand that is free, such as playing the piano, waving to people, spinning a hoop around your wrist, or eating an apple. I leave this experimentation to your own creative urges.

Lesson 23: One-and-One, Two-and-One

This lesson will cover the One-and-One *exercises,* which involve two balls in two hands, and the Two-and-One *variations,* which involve three balls. Don't confuse the title of the last lesson, "Two-Ball Juggling," with the "Two-and-One" of this lesson.

The work you will be doing with the One-and-One is not strictly juggling. Remember that juggling is defined as having more objects in the air than there are hands involved.

Unison Exercise. "One-and-One" means that there is one ball in each hand. Pop both balls up at exactly the same time, and in unison, catch them in the same hands. Throw them to the same height over and over again, keeping the rhythm as even as possible. Practice using various heights, but you should always make sure that the two balls go to the same height. When you are doing it right, you will get the feeling that the two balls are connected to each other by some kind of invisible rod as they go up and down together.

Alternating Exercise. This is similar to the Unison Exercise, except that each hand waits, so that as one ball comes down into your left hand, you throw the other ball straight up with your right. The effect is like the motion of a seesaw. The rhythm is similar to that of Two-Ball juggling, except that each ball remains in its own hand.

Criss-Cross Exercise. This has the same basic rhythm as the Unison, except that here you throw both balls at the same time across to your opposite hands, instead of to the same hands. Mid-air collisions are a possibility. With a little experimentation, you can learn to throw

one of the balls, preferably the one from your right or better hand, just a little higher than the other. Since a higher throw will take just a little longer to travel, you should throw this ball a fraction of a second earlier than usual, and catch it a fraction of a second later. This timing is instinctive in any case, and will come to you with a little practice. Another way to avoid collisions is to throw the balls a little forward and back of one another, which you can do once you have really good control of your pattern.

Collision Exercise. Don't get too good at the "Criss-Cross" exercise before working on the "Collision" exercise, where the idea is to make the balls collide. If you throw the balls carefully enough, you can make them hit dead-on, and they will bounce back down into the same hands they came from. If they don't hit just right, they will have a forward-and-back bounce and be very hard to recover. This exercise is more likely to succeed if you use the Narrow Pattern, especially in the beginning.

TWO-AND-ONE VARIATIONS

After you have mastered the One-and-One Exercises, especially the Unison, you will be ready to work on the "Two-and-One Variations." These involve three balls. They were not described with the rest of the Three-Ball work because the Two-and-One rhythm is the same as the Two- and Four-Ball rhythm. Two balls are thrown straight up at the same time, one from each hand. Then a third ball, which will be called the "Alternating Ball," is thrown as the first two come down. The rhythm is an alternating one, like Two-Ball juggling. The Two-and-One is a kind of hybrid of Two-Ball and Three-Ball work—three balls being juggled with the rhythm of two.

Two-And-One Conceptualization. This kind of juggling can be thought of in two different ways. It is either the Unison Exercise with an extra Alternating Ball in one hand going in an alternating rhythm with the other two, as just described (since this ball is separated from the other two by rhythm or time, this conceptualization is called "Time Separation"), or it can also be thought of as Two-Ball juggling in one hand, with an extra ball (dubbed an "Odd Ball" to avoid confusion) in the other hand. This ball is going in Unison with just one of the other two balls. Since this Odd Ball is in the other hand, separated from the other two by space, this conceptualization is called "Space Separation."

In summary, you have an Alternating Ball in Time Separation, or an Odd Ball in Space Separation. It doesn't really matter which way you look at them, since they are but two different ways of looking at the same thing. However, sometimes one and sometimes the other approach will greatly simplify what is happening, both in this lesson and in the lesson on Four Balls.

TIME SEPARATION

In Time Separation, the main variations will be the Parallel and the Criss-Cross. In the Parallel variations, I will cover the Umbrella and Scoop movements and the Double Um-

Parallel. Think of this variation as being made up of a Unison and an Alternating Ball. The Alternating Ball is going up and down in the same hand as one of the other two balls. Recall the Tray-Plane points, and observe that this Alternating Ball can be thrown up and down from any one of the four points. In terms of these points, the Unison balls themselves are thrown from the Left-Center and Right-Center points, respectively. The location of the Alternating Ball determines the particular sub-variation of the Two-and-One Parallel you are doing.

(1) Left-Outside: The Alternating Ball is going up and down parallel to the left-hand ball, alternating with it, to the left of your left hand.

(2) Left-Inside: The Alternating Ball is to the right of the other ball in your left hand, still thrown by your left hand.

(3) Right-Inside: The Alternating Ball is to the left of the ball in your right hand, now being thrown by your right hand.

(4) Right-Outside: The Alternating Ball is to the right of the ball in your right hand.

Remember that each ball in each of these variations has its own column in which to travel up and down. In all Parallel variations, a ball is never thrown over or under any other but is always traveling next to another ball.

Umbrella and Scoop Movements. To change from one Parallel variation to another, you have to throw the Alternating Ball over or under another ball. To do this use the Umbrella or the Scoop, both covered in the lesson on Two-Ball juggling. With the Umbrella, just throw the Alternating Ball over to another Tray-Plane point, and then keep it there in its new spot for a while. Continue to work on this until you can throw the Alternating Ball smoothly over in either direction to neighboring Tray-Plane points. Soon you will be able to skip over one point, and eventually you will be able to throw with ease directly from the Left-Outside point to the Right-Outside point, or the other way.

The Scoop Movement is a little more limited, since you can only scoop between two points in the same hand. The basic Scoops are from the Right-Outside point to the Right-Inside, and then vice versa, and between the same points in your left hand. In both Umbrella and Scoop, the use of a red ball will help both you and those watching to follow the movements of the Alternating Ball.

Double Umbrella Movement. By using the Umbrella Movement as described, you can move the Alternating Ball back and forth along the four Tray-Plane points. Move it one position each time you throw it. The result will be two balls making vertical motions (the Unison), while the Alternating Ball is making three separate little arcs over the others. The middle arc will not be over a ball, but over the space between your two hands. If you bring your hands a little closer together, and leave this arc out, you will have a genuine Double Umbrella, with two arcs.

Criss-Cross Variation. The Unison is involved in each of the variations described in the section on Time Separation. Therefore it would seem possible, on paper at least, to substitute the Criss-Cross or Collision Exercise for the Unison anywhere that it appears. Some of these variations will be harder than others—for instance, the Double-Umbrella Movement combined with the Collision.

SPACE SEPARATION

After you have mastered the variations in the section on Time Separation, you can go on to some variations having a Space Separation. These are the Cyclic variations.

Two-and-One Cyclic. Here we consider the two balls in the same hand as the basic unit. (In the unit called the Unison, you had one ball in each hand.) This basic unit consists of two balls going around each other in a cyclic path. There are two basic variations on each side: Either your right hand does Inside-Cyclic–Two-Ball juggling while your left hand throws the Odd Ball up and down in unison with one of the two balls in the Cycle, or you can do all this with an Outside-Cyclic pattern.

Two-and-One Faking. This variation can be seen equally well either as a Time Separation or a Space Separation. In your right hand, juggle two balls parallel to one another, and throw the Odd Ball in your left hand up in unison with one of these first two. Now you have the choice of either throwing the Odd Ball or just holding it in your hand. A kind of "fake," or optical illusion, is possible here. If you keep the Odd Ball out on your fingertips and carry it up with your hand instead of throwing it, you can make it move exactly as if it had been thrown. Turn your hand toward those watching in such a way that they see very little of your fingers, and they won't be able to tell whether you are throwing the ball or not.

Another related variation is to hold on to the ball for a throw occasionally, so it is paired with one or the other of the two balls in your right hand. By using brightly colored balls, you can create some nice effects.

Two-and-One vs. Three-Ball Juggling. To change back and forth between Two-and-One and Cascade juggling (a Cascade Transition), start by doing some Cascade juggling. Just before you are about to throw a ball with your right hand, bring that hand in closer to your centerline, on it if possible, and throw that ball straight up in the middle, a little higher than normal. When it starts to come down, throw the other two balls, one from each hand, up at the same time. You are now doing a Two-and-One Parallel. The first ball is thrown higher than usual since you must do two throws in succession from your right hand during the Transition.

The Transition back from Two-and-One to the Cascade is done by throwing the Alternating Ball over to the outside of your opposite hand. The ball in that hand is thrown next, under the incoming ball, and you are off into the Regular Cascade. For instance, if you were throwing the Alternating Ball (in the center, here) with your right hand, you would throw it to the left of your left hand to get back into the Cascade. Your right hand would have to wait a little longer than normal between throws during the transition.

Two-and-One Practice. Work on these basic points of Two-and-One juggling: the Unison, Alternating, Criss-Cross, and Collision Exercises; and the Two-and-One Parallel, Umbrella and Scoop Movements, the Double Umbrella, Criss-Cross, Cyclic, Faking, and Transition variations. These are preparation for Four-Ball juggling. There is some opportunity here for your own explorations. Sometimes it is easier to work out the more complicated variations on paper, and then see if you can do them. Your body itself is a poor innovator; it usually wants to be left alone to do what it likes. By planning things out ahead of time, and putting down on paper what you want to do, you can challenge your body to break out of its lazy, confining habit patterns.

Lesson 24: Four Balls

Before you attempt to work with four balls, you should be proficient in all the One-and-One exercises and Two-and-One variations given in the preceding lesson. Review that lesson carefully. Four-Ball juggling is a direct extension of the Two-and-One work.

Ball-Hand Rule. There is a rule in juggling that the number of balls plus the number of hands involved in a pattern must be an odd number. This is certainly the case with Two-Ball juggling—two balls plus one hand equals three, which is an odd number. In the Regular Cascade, three balls plus two hands equals five. In Four Balls this would go as follows: four balls plus one hand (or three hands) equals five (or seven). The additional hand is necessary to keep the total odd. Since you don't have three hands, and since doing four balls with one hand is a little advanced at this point, there must be some way of doing four balls with *two* hands (equals six) without violating the rule. The answer is to break the pattern into two equal parts of two independent sets of two balls each, one set for each hand. Each of these now obeys the rule of two balls plus one hand.

In fact, most Four-Ball juggling is nothing more than two independent sets of two balls in each hand. The only variations that do not conform are the ones in which there is a simultaneous trade of balls from one hand to the other (the One-and-One Criss-Cross) or complex patterns where the timing is badly lopsided. These variations go beyond the scope of this book.

Conceptualization. There are two possible ways of seeing Four-Ball juggling, just as there were two ways of seeing the Two-and-One. They are (1) If you cut the pattern in half with a vertical line, you will have what I was just talking about—two units of Two-Ball juggling, one in each hand, separated by space. This is similar to the situation with the Odd Ball in the previous lesson. (2) If you cut the pattern into two halves with a horizontal line, you will have two units of one-and-one, which are separated by time, as was the Alternating Ball in the last lesson. The One-and-One Criss-Cross is another pattern that can be substituted here.

SPACE SEPARATION

By making a space separation, and considering your two hands independently, as you did in the two units of Two-Ball juggling, you will discover that you can combine any pattern in your left hand with any pattern in your right. For instance, you can have a Parallel-Parallel, an Inside-Inside, or an Outside-Outside combination. There are also mixed combinations, such as Inside-Parallel, and so on.

Parallel-Parallel. If you combine a Parallel pattern in your left hand with one in your right, you will still have two choices. They are (1) The *Scissors*. You can make your Right-Inside and Left-Inside throws in unison, and alternate this with the two Outside throws in unison. Your arms, like a pair of scissors, will go toward and then away from one another. (2) The *Washing Machine*. You can make your Left-Outside in unison with your Right-Inside, and then throw the remaining Left-Inside with the Right-Outside. Both your hands are making throws at the same time from points to the left of their center positions, alternating with throws from points to the right of their normal center positions. Your two hands will be moving together to your left and right as you do this, creating a feeling of rotating your shoulders or your whole body as a washing machine does. Try to avoid any actual movement. Keep your energy in your hands, and out of your body.

Cyclic Combinations. These are combinations of the cyclic variations of Two-Ball juggling, which you learned before. They include the Inside-Inside and the Outside-Outside. In each, your hands work like gear wheels, making two circles in opposite directions, coming together and going apart symmetrically. This is different from the Egg-Beater, where your hands came together, but in alternating rhythm so that one hand arrives first and leaves before the other one arrives.

Fountain, or Inside-Inside. In this combination, all balls are thrown up from the Inside points of the Tray Plane and fall down at the Outside points. The throws of the individual units are outward at an angle over the other balls, producing a cyclic rotation. All balls follow the same path, one after the other.

Reverse Fountain, or Outside-Outside. This is just the reverse of the above. The balls are thrown from the Outside points of the Tray Plane, similar to the Overthrow covered in the lesson on the Reverse Cascade.

Locomotive Patterns. In these patterns, you do a combination of an Inside and an Outside. The result is two clockwise rotations together, like the two linked wheels of a locomotive. These patterns may be done in counterclockwise rotations, too. Once you can get each hand to do these variations independently, try the remaining combinations. Since there are three patterns for each hand, you have a total of nine combinations to work on, including the ones I have already covered.

Umbrella and Scoop Patterns. If you can do an Umbrella or a Scoop with either hand, then you should be able to use this pattern in combination with the same or different pattern in your other hand. I am not saying that this is easy; it is one of those "paper variations" that can become a reality if you work hard enough.

Alternating Rhythm. Up to now, you have been throwing balls in unison—that is, balls leave your left hand and your right hand at the same time. After you have these patterns in their unison forms and can sustain them, you should try them with Alternating Rhythm. Do exactly the same thing with each hand that you did before, using any variation you have already done. The only difference is that here you start with your right hand first and quickly alternate the throws. This makes the corresponding throws in your left hand half a beat later than the throws in your right. You can also use this Alternating Rhythm in the Two-and-One variations, except where the Criss-Cross is involved. Visually, this breaks up the sameness and symmetry of the pattern and makes it "look harder," even though it is just about as easy as regular Four-Ball juggling.

TIME SEPARATION

Four-Ball Criss-Cross. By visualizing Four-Ball juggling as two sets of One-and-One, you can then substitute a One-and-One Criss-Cross anytime you are simultaneously throwing from your right and left hands.

Four-Ball Practice. For a practice exercise, write down all the Four-Ball variations that you have mastered, and pin the sheet to the wall. Then do the whole list, going from one to the other, without missing or stopping. Rewrite the list in some other order, and do it again. If you drop a ball, go into the Two-and-One variations. If you drop another, go into Two-Ball juggling. If you should drop still another ball, throw the last ball really high, catch it, spin around, and go into a deep bow. Those watching will still applaud!

Lesson 25: Five Balls

In juggling parlance what is called The Numbers Game is an attempt by some jugglers to get the greatest possible number of objects going at the same time. My own experience has been that if you are doing three objects and there are people watching, they will inevitably ask, "Can you do four?" So you learn to do four and they ask, "Can you do five?" And if you spend a year of hard work learning to do five, they will blithely ask, "Can you do six?"

Seeing how human nature is, it might be better not to get involved in the Numbers Game at all. It seems to be a kind of dead end. No satisfactory place is reached with it, and some of the greatest jugglers in the world have almost lost their sanity by getting too hung up on how many objects they could handle successfully. There are, as you have seen, plenty of things to do with just three objects, no more than three and no less. The satisfaction in the Numbers Game comes from the appreciation you will get from other jugglers who understand the work involved. You will become a juggler's juggler. Doing five balls in any case is a nice, hefty chunk of work, a kind of magnum opus for those who want a challenge. For that reason I will cover it in this lesson.

Five Balls vs. Three Balls. When you juggle five balls, the path or orbit of the balls is identical to that of three balls. The difference is that there are now two more balls moving around that path. Because the track is more crowded, the pattern has to be higher to make a little more room between the balls. Another difference is that you have to throw the balls more often from each hand, since they are closer together. Both the higher pattern and the more rapid firing require additional amounts of energy and more accuracy in your throws.

Before you start on Five Balls, work through the following simpler exercises. They will help bridge the distance between where you are now with three balls and where you are headed with five.

Cascade Flash. Start by juggling three balls

in a very low pattern, just as you have done many times before. Then, in mid-volley, throw all three balls up into a high pattern in Quick Succession (right-left-right). Since the lower pattern is much faster, the three balls will be fired off quickly. The first ball thrown will still be on its way up as the second and even third balls are thrown. The result of this will be a moment when all three balls are in the air at the same time, before the first ball lands again. For a moment, your hands will be totally empty. At this point you might clap your hands together, as proof of this fact. Then catch the balls in the same order that you threw them (with left, right, and left hands catching) and go back into Low Pattern again.

Make sure that you throw from a very low pattern into a very high one. The rhythm of the movement should be THROW • THROW • THROW(clap) • CATCH • CATCH • CATCH. When you can do this five times in a row perfectly, switch hands and begin to throw a Quick Succession from your left hand first (left-right-left). As you improve, do the "Cascade Flash" starting from the very first ball thrown, rather than from the middle of the volley.

Slots. What you have just been doing is throwing three balls into three of the five available places in the Five-Ball juggling pattern. These places will be referred to as "Slots." If you visualize a path with the five slots moving around on it, you will see that each slot comes to one hand, is thrown, and comes to the other. Your aim here is to gradually fill these slots with balls.

As soon as you start your volley, the slots immediately start moving around the large Five-Ball path, even though the balls themselves are still in your low three-ball pattern. That means you have to throw them rapidly ahead so they can catch up with their slots; in Five-Ball work, the first few throws are faster. As soon as every ball finds its own slot, the rhythm slows down into an even pace.

From now on in this lesson, you will be dealing with five balls. It might be better to get some smaller balls if you have trouble getting three balls into either hand. The first objective

is to get used to having the additional balls in your hands.

Grab. Make a Basket in your left hand and place two balls in it. A Basket, you'll remember, is formed by placing one ball in the center of your hand and a second ball on your fingertips. The Grab is what you do with your right hand in order to hold three balls. You don't just reach out and grab them, but that's what

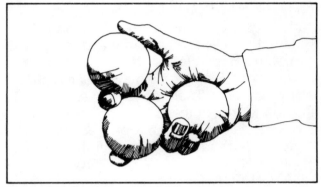

Three-Ball Grab for Five-Ball juggling

it feels like. Place one ball in the palm of your right hand and a second one on your fingertips, just as if you were making a Basket. Now push this fingertip ball over toward your little finger. Place the third ball between your thumb and your index finger, touching the ball you just pushed over. This last ball inserted is the first one you'll be throwing.

One Throw. Put three balls in your right hand in a Grab and two in your left hand in a Basket. Open up the Basket into a Grab, leaving an empty space for the third ball. Now throw the ball from the Grab in your right hand to the Grab in your left. The catch here is very tricky, and will take some work to perfect. If the third ball keeps bouncing out, try to have this ball hit your fingers first, before touching the other ball. Another thing you can do is really let your hand "give" as the ball comes in. This has the effect of slowing down its relative speed of arrival. Keep working on this until you have no problem catching or throwing, and you can throw this ball into a high path.

Three Balls and Two Riders. After you have become proficient at doing one throw, move on to two and three throws. All you have to do is pretend that the first or palm ball in each hand is not there, or is a part of your hand, and juggle the remaining three balls as in the Regular Cascade. The extra two balls in your palms are called "Riders," since they are just along "for the ride"; they are not thrown. Keep going with this until you can juggle with these three balls as if the other two were not there at all. Catching with the Grab is the trickiest part of this, and it takes real concentration and hard work.

Three-Ball Flash. In this step you will be combining two previous exercises, the Cascade Flash and the Three-Balls and Two-Riders. Place all five balls in the starting position, with a Basket in your left hand and a Grab in your right. Start juggling three of the balls in a low pattern. Then do a Cascade Flash, throwing three of these balls up into the high Five-Ball path. Catching won't be easy. The rhythm is the same as the one for the Cascade Flash: THROW • THROW • THROW • CATCH • CATCH • CATCH.

Catch. This is called a Three-Ball Flash, but it really means that three balls out of five are being flashed. Once you have this exercise, you will be very close to being able to do Five-Ball juggling. Each of the steps in this lesson is enormous, so be patient, and don't rush things.

Although you have done a lot of learning and a lot of juggling by this time, you will find that most of your experience is of relatively little help here. Try to approach learning Five Balls almost as if you had never juggled before. Make sure you can do these three exercises: the Cascade Flash, the Three-Balls and Two-Riders, and the Three-Ball Flash, which is a combination of the first two. You can also work on doing these at the beginning of your volley, which is harder than going into it in the middle. Work until you feel really comfortable.

Four-Ball Flash. Before you try this, you should do the Three-Ball Flash many times in a row to warm up and psyche yourself up. Then do another Four-Ball Flash, but let a fourth ball go up into the pattern, and catch it. If your Three-Ball Flash started with a Quick Succession of throws starting from your right hand (right-left-right), then the fourth throw will be from your left hand again. Here the

rhythm will be THROW • THROW • THROW • EXCHANGE • CATCH • CATCH • CATCH. The first of the four catches is not shown because it combines with the fourth throw to form an Exchange. Be sure that you wait for the first throw to almost come down to your left hand before throwing the fourth ball (the second throw from your left hand) as part of that Exchange. Work on this until you can do it well, then switch to the other side, throwing left, right, left, and right. The Exchange will now be on your right. Keep going back to the Three-Ball Flash or other exercises if you have trouble and need to stabilize your pattern. As before, begin by doing this Flash in mid-volley. Later you can work up to doing it from a dead start.

Catching will become increasingly important as you progress. In the Four-Ball Flash, you will be throwing two balls from each hand. Your right hand, where you have the fifth remaining unthrown ball, will have to handle two more balls coming in. You will have to catch the first of these well enough that you will be immediately ready to catch the other one as it arrives. Do not go past this step until you can do it perfectly in either direction five times in a row.

Five-Ball Flash. Now we are coming to the inevitable endpoint of this lesson and, in one sense, of the work in this book. If you have done everything carefully up to now, you should be able to learn the Five-Ball Flash, flashing all five balls starting with the low pattern of the Cascade. All you have to do is throw that last remaining ball into the high path when its turn comes. The throws will now be right, left, right, left, and right. The last two throws will be part of Exchanges, so you will be throwing the second ball in your left hand as the first comes in from your right, then the third ball in your right hand as the first ball comes in from your left. The rhythm will be THROW • THROW • THROW • EXCHANGE • EXCHANGE • CATCH • CATCH • CATCH. The last two throws overlap the first two catches as Exchanges.

After a while you will be able to pick up five balls and go into various flashes—three, four, and five. There is no reason to stop there, since the first ball has come around again. Continue building with six, seven, and eight flashes. Eventually, you will lose count of the number of throws, and be juggling five balls indefinitely. Until then, try to set a definite number of throws, do them, and stop.

Variations. Five-Ball juggling does not lend itself to variations. There is too much need for attention and energy on the part of the juggler to add any fancy stuff. Also, the people watching will be satisfied just to see you do five balls, at least for a while. Therefore, there is little reason to go into variations. Also, you will have very little time for such things. To get the necessary time you would have to throw the balls seven or eight feet up, which would require even more of your energy and decrease your accuracy.

The Reverse Cascade is about the only possible variation with Five Balls. Start with the overthrows on one side, then on the other, and then on both, as you did with three balls.

POSTSCRIPT

I just want to say a word about the club and hoop equivalents of the Advanced Ball Juggling you have just been studying. With clubs, you can continue on to doing Two Clubs, Two-and-One, and Four Clubs. Even Five Clubs is possible, although I have seen professional jugglers literally spend weeks and months trying to get it and sustain it. For Two-Club juggling, it is easier to throw the clubs as Doubles. For all the more advanced forms, Doubles are just about essential to get the needed time. High, slow Singles are possible, but they lack energy and are hard to regulate properly.

Hoops also lend themselves to these patterns, especially with large numbers of them. To hold three hoops in one hand, you have to stick each hoop between a different finger so that each one will be ready to throw without hesitation.

This book deals with what I call "Mainstream Juggling," rather than with the specialties or personal variations that a particular juggler may spend years perfecting. When I talk about mainstream juggling I mean those variations that every juggler should work on until he or she becomes proficient. After that, each person can develop in his own direction. You might, for example, decide to juggle pots or pans, or cups or plates, or knives or forks. Perhaps your preferences run to pillows and handkerchiefs, or eggs. An unlimited number of specialties are possible.

This ends my formal instruction on juggling variations. A lot has been left open for you to pursue. I would appreciate your communicating with me, through the publisher, about any discoveries you have made, so that I can someday present them to the juggling community, and everyone can learn them.

V. Performing And Teaching

Lesson 26: Notes on Performing

Your mystic path along the Way of Juggling is not yet over. Once you have mastered all the techniques and incorporated them into your body, heart, and soul, and when you have established them in your subconscious, you should consider sharing with others what you have experienced.

Get together some nice brightly colored equipment. It should be flashy, since color attracts attention and adds a great deal to what you are doing. Work by yourself, gradually developing a sequence of material according to your own natural inclinations. Generally, the progression should be from simple to difficult, from low energy to high, and from solo work to partner work. Some people find it advantageous to make a list of the variations they will perform, since it is very easy to forget a lot of things when you are performing for people. Get yourself a large knapsack or canvas duffle bag to carry your equipment. A lot of jugglers use suitcases. You will find that as you do more and more juggling, you will acquire more equipment, which will soon overflow the largest suitcase. (Besides, I think suitcases are kind of straight.) When performing, it is best to leave everything inside your bag so that you can reach in and pull out "surprises" for your audience.

Begin performing gradually. Start with friends who are learning to juggle. Later, you can juggle for other friends, family, and neighbors. The next time there is a picnic or a party, get everybody together and juggle for them. If possible, you should always warm up for twenty minutes, preferably alone, before letting anyone watch you. It is always better to juggle where your audience can sit and watch, rather than where they have to stand or come and go from your performing. Get people to gather around you in a close circle. This is especially important in ball juggling, since much of the intricacy of it is lost if people are too far away from you. Don't perform your variations for as long as you would practice them; eight or ten seconds is enough for any one cycle. Use a clock to determine what you can do in this time. Next, you might want to go to a park to do your thing. Remember that while everybody thinks juggling is for children —parents always encourage their kids to watch the performance—it is really more of an adult entertainment, since children have a hard time appreciating the difficulty of what you are doing. From the standpoint of an adult audience, juggling is almost an intellectual entertainment much like music, chess, and mathematics.

PERFORMING BLOCKS

Physical Blocks. As you expand your juggling performing—working at schools, recreation centers, senior citizens' centers, birthday parties, bazaars, and all such things — you will encounter various physical situations. Outdoors, in particular, presents some problems. If the sky is bright, your high juggling work may suffer. If there is a strong wind, you will find that the objects, particularly lightweight ones like clubs, have a tendency to blow away as you juggle them. About the easiest way to deal with this problem is to stand facing the wind so that the clubs are blown toward you. Even better, stand with your back to the wind so that your body acts as a shield. Another possible answer is to make heavier clubs, but don't make them so heavy that you are deprived of the lightness and speed essential to juggling. Another outdoor complication is rain. I have juggled in the rain many times, and I can offer no special hints. Just juggle in the rain if you feel like it. (I have walked on stilts in deep snow and even juggled snowballs.

The major problems indoors are usually finding enough space in which to work and enough room to throw high and to let things drop without bonking the first row of spectators or breaking antiques. Also, lighting can be a problem indoors. Usually it is too dark indoors to see well enough to juggle. If you are fortunate enough to be on a lighted stage, you will probably be blinded by spotlights.

Audience Blocks. You may find it difficult at first to juggle before an audience. You may have a problem getting people's attention before you get going. You may feel foolish and embarrassed. You may feel a sudden lack of motivation just as you are about to begin performing (Why am I doing this?). You may forget half the things you planned to do. You may be disturbed by the look on someone's face, or by some remark, especially when someone you know is involved. A noise, or a child or a pet running around between your legs, or some other activity in the same area you are working in can be a serious or insurmountable distraction. You may respond by getting flustered, start to make mistakes, drop your juggling props and have to retrieve them from the audience. All of these experiences, while potentially major or minor "disasters," are in reality very useful learning experiences, whose value go far beyond the immediate need to put on a good "show." Overcoming them will help you open up your whole personality, and give you a more philosophical and relaxed outlook on life.

Ego Blocks. Another area where you might find difficulty is in the ego involvement of what you are doing. Regardless of what you do in your performing, some people will always react to you out of *their* ego, as though you were coming on with a lot of yours. They may call out, "*I* can do that," or "That's not so hard." There is no point in challenging these people. You have to be careful that the message you are putting out is not: "Look what I can do that you can't," but rather something on this order: "This magic is part of the infinite variety of manifestations in the universe; let's celebrate together." Or something like that.

If people come up to you and say, "Let's see if I can do that," it is better for you to discourage them. It is never a good idea to lend anyone your equipment. It is yours; you made it; and it has your vibration on it. It is another matter if they are seriously interested in becoming your students.

Center. Another important factor in performing, which relates to much of what I have already touched upon, is the creation and maintenance of a center within you. At first, you may use an external center, such as your objects, or a particular member of the audience, as a focus for your attention and energies. Later, you will become more aware of your inner center, a place from which you derive your energy and to which you direct your consciousness. You can think of this as being in a specific location within your body, if you like. Some people claim that it is in their solar plexus, in the pit of the stomach. Others think of it as being near the heart, since this is the point at which the nerves and communication lines from the arms join the spinal cord. Once you have really located this place, and are in a centered state, you can juggle anywhere, at any time.

Energy. Once the people in your audience have warmed up to you, they will start to give you a lot of energy. This is really a fine feeling, but a couple of pitfalls can arise because of it. If you are getting too much energy from your audience so that you become receptive and responsive to it, you may get "excited" and let that extra energy creep into your juggling. This can be helpful up to a point, but if you don't exercise control over the incoming energy, it may wreak havoc with your internal tuning. It may make you unable to keep your rhythm, hold on to the balls, or do certain variations. For instance, you may find yourself overturning the clubs, throwing the balls too high, or misjudging distances. In other words, you are getting too much of a good thing.

Conversely, too little energy from your audience will leave you with the arduous task of "entertaining" them. In either case, dependence on audience energy is a risky business. A third choice is for you to be your own storehouse of energy on which you can draw whenever you need it.

Actor-Audience Duality. Entertaining means setting yourself up on the opposite side of some kind of wall, creating a distance between you and your audience. A kind of subject-object duality is created. You put yourself on display as some kind of phenomenon. This has been especially true of the classic jugglers, about whom I have said very little.

"Being" with your audience is another alternative. Call the audience your "friends." Being with them means that you are all sharing the same energy. Stand close to them, not up on a stage, so you have a chance to watch them, enjoy them, and see them as people, not just a sea of blank faces who only act and react as a group. If you respond to them as individuals, they can respond to you that way. This "being with your friends" is about as close as you can get to a state of egoless performing, which marks the true juggling master.

If you stay in that state of being with your friends long and often enough, while "performing" you may find that at some point your friends out there will start to do the juggling. They will feed you with energy, which your body will automatically channel into juggling. As you work, you send the energy back to them, and it keeps circling around and around. You find yourself standing there, letting it happen, without any effort or will of your own. Being able to be with your audience in this state of awareness, even for a short time, is one of the great rewards of the hard work you have invested in perfecting your juggling ability.

A Path. Finally, for those who wish to do so, juggling can be pursued as a part of your spiritual unfoldment. But unlike an actual path, with definitely stated points along it, the juggling path can only be seen and experienced one moment at a time. That moment is *now.* Now I do this. Now I do that. How I will be juggling a month from now is of no concern to me. Why I am doing it and Where it will lead me are concerns that will only get in the way of what's happening right now. The point is to do the task at hand carefully and keep your whole attention focused on it. A time will come when it will just happen. You can't start there, however. You have to work up to that point. When you get there, you will realize that there is nothing to "figure out" in practicing the exercises—there is only *doing* and *watching.* At a later stage, there will only be watching. Ultimately, you will be aware only that what you are really doing is putting out great quantities of love to the people you are with, and you won't have any notion at all of objects flying around you.

Lesson 27: Teaching the Carlo Method

Teaching juggling is the completion of your learning cycle. But at the same time, it is the beginning of a new cycle, which starts at that moment when you can begin to transmit your knowledge and ability to others. It should go without saying that I consider this book to be a very valuable aid in doing that teaching. However, any book, no matter how carefully it is put together, is not enough; you can't just *read* yourself into being a juggler, you have to *do* it. It's even better if you have some other jugglers to work with, and the best of all is to have a live teacher.

You can be this live teacher for your friends. Have them read this book, just a little bit at a time, and go through the corresponding exercises. You should be working closely with them as they do this. Remember that you have been through the same exercises and have encountered obstacles that they will encounter, and because of this you can be of great help to them. Of course you can be of obvious help when it comes to doing partner work such as passing, take-aways, give-aways, drop-downs, etc. Half Juggling is especially useful to the beginning student. Throughout this book many hints have been given which are of as much use to a teacher as to the student.

Psychological Factors. As you work with your students, you should be aware of not only the physical level on which they are operating, but also their individual psychological needs. Ask yourself: What are their inner states? How do they feel about what they are doing? Would they rather be somewhere else? Are their minds interfering with the task at hand? Do they trust and have confidence in their teacher? Will they do what you say? Are their bodies tense? Is their breathing constricted? Will they let themselves learn, or are they trying not to learn for some reason? How can you, the teacher, get them to be in better control of their bodies and themselves? What areas of work should you assign them, and how fast should you take them? There is an enormous amount that a teacher should be conscious of in this work, aside from making sure that the students adhere strictly to the details of each exercise.

The exercises in this book are presented the way they are for one reason only: *They work.* They have produced good jugglers, who have gone deeply into the advanced areas of juggling, but who are also flexible and have the ability to keep adding new material to their store of skills. Some people I know have mastered the Regular Cascade in a few days, or even in as little as a couple of hours, using the Carlo Method. But before you teach the Carlo Method, make sure that you know it well yourself. You should understand with your head and experience with your body something of the reasons behind each instruction given. Much explanation has been given at various places throughout the book, and you have your own stock of experience to draw from as well.

How good a juggler do you have to be before you begin to teach? I would say that you should work hard on the exercises and should sincerely attempt everything given in the mainstream topics covered. Teaching is basically a skill in its own right. If you have some understanding of what happens in the teaching and learning process, then you are well-equipped to teach juggling, or anything else. You can even teach people how to do things beyond your own level of skill. Some of my own students have come up with amazing and original variations, and I have included some of them in this book.

You will no doubt find that the second you start teaching, you will become aware of your own inadequacies, and this will spur you on to do more work on yourself. It is the constant demand made on you by your students to help them and to always know what to say and do that will keep you working, not only to stay ahead of them but also to improve your own juggling, and also perhaps to hit upon new and better ways of teaching it to them.

Lesson 28: Summary

The topics covered in this book have been arranged in a very definite order so each section prepares you for the next one. You have been taken into the work, not haphazardly, but according to a definite plan.

The first thing is the basic orientation and position of your body (and mind). This is the foundation upon which you will build all the rest of your work. Next, you are given the Self-Checking Methods so you can become your own teacher and catch yourself, observing just what is happening with your juggling. Without this attention to what you are doing, there can be no real learning.

After this come the lessons involving the Cascade Progression, with increasing numbers of throws—up to four. As you progress in numbers of throws, you will find comments on the problems that arise at each level. In doing One Throw you learn the Cup position of your hand. In Two Throws, there is the Basket Position and the Exchange, with its pathways, timing, and accent. Three Throws is mainly an amplification of the work of Two Throws, but on the opposite side. In Four Throws, repetition and Drift are new elements to be dealt with, and you are now ready to do a continuous Regular Cascade.

Once the Cascade is going, you should begin to explore it and see what its limits and boundaries are. Half-juggling is given here as an aid to working with a partner as soon as possible. Eye-independence exercises help you to free your attention for other things. Another way to help you expand your abilities at this point is to explore the size of your pattern: large, small, high, low, wide, or narrow.

Once your Regular Cascade is fairly solid, you can combine it with various Body Positions while executing certain Body Movements. Although so far you have concentrated on keeping the rest of your body still, now you can move it again, this time consciously and under control.

Next come the Overthrow and the resulting Reverse Cascade, which is the other half of the work on the Underthrow that you have been doing up to this time. This completes the possible palm-up throws and catches from Home Position. This lesson also serves to introduce, informally, the Full-Shower Progression technique as a way of building up the frequency of any special throw. This progression is also a preparation for the rest of the elementary ball work, including Passing. The Same-Hand throw prepares you for Wall Bouncing and Passing.

In the next lesson, on Clawing, you work on throwing and catching with your palm down, and also sideways, completing all the basic throws and catches in Home Position. Clawing is preparation for Bounce work, Beginnings, Passing, and Take-Aways.

Work on Body Throws comes next because of the physical exertion and control needed. Also the departure from Home Position required for body throws would have been too upsetting earlier, before that position had become well established.

This is followed by Bounce work. Bouncing is instinctive, easy, and fun, and it has been delayed for just that reason. Your juggling must be well established so you can bring more consciousness to the Bouncing and not regard it as just a plaything. Wall Bounces are a direct preparation for Ball Passing.

The other Beginnings, which depend on Clawing, can now be given. The Endings come just before the lessons on Passing so you and your partner can end simultaneously with a flourish, and you can gauge how closely the two of you come to juggling in true harmony.

Ball Passing is the culmination of Cascade Ball work, and takes you into a whole new level of awareness. You are now adjusting everything you have learned to an outside influence or force in the form of your partner. After this, there is a lesson on Ball-Passing variations to help you solidify what you have just learned.

Finally come the Take-Aways and Give-Aways. These also use Clawing, and are placed here because in order to do them you must first experience the attunement and ad-

justing process with a partner, which is best learned in the Ball-Passing lessons.

Once these ball-juggling areas have been learned thoroughly, you should go immediately into clubs, avoiding for the moment any additional work in ball juggling. Much of what you have learned with balls will translate immediately into clubs, if you don't allow interference from other work having a different rhythm.

The lessons on clubs follow the same development as those on ball work. Lesson 17 recaps the chapter on Cascade Juggling and Lessons 1 through 6. Lesson 18 quickly goes over Lessons 7 through 11. Lesson 12 has no club equivalent. Lesson 19 corresponds to Lesson 13, with some new material unique to clubs. Lesson 20 takes up Lessons 14 through 16, with emphasis on the differences between balls and clubs. At this point in the work, the carryover from balls to clubs should be fairly apparent to you, and you should be working more on your own, creating a club variation for each ball variation that you learned.

Hoops are the third major type of juggling object. Since by the time you get to hoops, you have now been over the basic areas twice —once with balls and once with clubs—hoops are treated very briefly. Only when techniques differ radically from those you learned for balls and clubs do I discuss them in any detail. At this point we come to the end of the three-object work in the Cascade Rhythm.

In the lessons on Advanced Ball juggling you are introduced to two other rhythms. These are left until this time to give you a chance to get as much as possible out of the Cascade work without being confused by alien vibrations.

The first of these two rhythms is just a simple alternation of two balls in one hand. This seesaw rhythm is basic to Lessons 22 through 24. Work on Two Balls, Two-and-One, and Four Balls trains you to work with two, three, and four objects, respectively, in this rhythm.

Five Balls is a separate topic, demanding all the experience and training you can muster. It is actually more like three-object work, with two extra throws added. It is the Master's work, and one of the areas that indisputably, in every person, requires many hours of hard work. One person in a hundred is a "natural" three-ball juggler. I have never seen a "natural" five-ball juggler.

This advanced ball work also has its equivalent in clubs and hoops. As the textbooks say, "This is left as an exercise for the student." There is probably as much work to be done with two, four, and five clubs and hoops as there is in all the rest of the work put together.

I have left the two chapters on Performing and Teaching until the very last. Performing should precede teaching. Both of these areas will test your knowledge and skill in juggling, and they will help you continue to grow. Performing puts a real strain on your skill, your centering, and your energy. Teaching requires you to reexamine everything you have learned in order to be able to explain *and* demonstrate it to another person and correct his errors.

I hope that this series of lessons has been a sort of adventure for you. By adventure, I mean that you go in *here,* and you come out *there;* you have become a changed person as a result of your experiences. If you worked carefully through this material, or even a good part of it, you, will have your own idea of what the Juggling Experience is. It is not something you have only heard about, or have read about; not even something you have seen; but something you have gotten inside of, and something that has gotten inside of you—a real experience that has become a part of your life and will stay with you forever.

About the Author

CARLO (Charles Lewis) has had a varied career. He graduated from Johns Hopkins University in Baltimore with a degree in geology and for five years taught math and science in public and private schools. More recently he has been a computer programmer, lighting designer for off-Broadway theaters, news announcer and writer for radio station WBAI in New York, and leader of an encounter group. Founder and original publisher of the *Gandalf Gazette,* a spiritual newspaper, he also edited the most recent edition of the widely circulated *Spiritual Community Guide.* He attended Hovey Burgess's Circus Arts Institute and founded his own performing group, the "Circus Minimus," also teaching juggling to Wall Streeters during lunch hours in Trinity Churchyard. Students of his are now teaching juggling in both New York and Los Angeles.